STRESS MANAGEMENT
FINDING THE BALANCE

Serendipity House / P.O. Box 1012 / Littleton, CO 80160

TOLL FREE 1-800-525-9563 / www.serendipityhouse.com

© 1989, 1999, 2000 Serendipity House. All rights reserved.

00 01 02 03 04 / **FN series•CHG** / 7 6 5 4 3 2 1

PROJECT ENGINEER
Lyman Coleman
Mike Shepherd

WRITING TEAM
Richard Peace, William Cutler, Andrew Sloan, Cathy Tardif

CARTOONS
Robert Schull

PRODUCTION TEAM
Christopher Werner, Sharon Penington, Erika Tiepel
The Serendipity Staff

ACKNOWLEDGMENTS

To Zondervan Bible Publishers
for permission to use
the NIV text, and Bible study notes
The Holy Bible, New International Bible Society.
© 1973, 1978, 1984 by International Bible Society.
Used by permission of Zondervan Bible Publishers.

Questions and Answers

1. **What is unique about this course?** The combination of three activities in one integrated program:
    ❐ Learning about the issue
    ❐ Interacting in small groups
    ❐ Studying the Bible

2. **Who is it for?**
    ❐ Home Bible Study groups
    ❐ Sunday school and other church groups
    ❐ Community organizations

3. **Where and how can I use this program?**
    ❐ Classrooms with movable chairs
    ❐ One-day seminars
    ❐ Weekend retreats
    ❐ Courses from seven to thirteen weeks

4. **How long is each session?** 90 minutes

5. **What if I do not have 90 minutes?** Divide sessions 1-6 into two sessions, making the course thirteen weeks instead of seven.

6. **How much does the course leader have to know about the subject?** Very little. This book provides all of the material. The leader convenes the meeting, makes introductory remarks, and follows the agenda.

7. **What about the group interaction?** This is directed by a Handout which each person is given at the beginning of the session. The Handout needs to be photocopied for every member. Another option is to provide each group member with his or her own course book (see page 5 for a detailed agenda to follow for each session).

8. **Why do you divide into subgroups of 4 to 6?** To allow everyone to share.

9. **How would you go about dividing the group?** Divide the number of participants in the group by 4 to 6 to determine the number of subgroups needed. Then, ask the group to count off—1, 2, 3, etc.

10. **Would you have the same groups meet every session?** That is up to you. There are advantages both ways.

11. **How does this course fit into the larger educational structures of the church?** This is an entry-level, short-term group for people with special needs or specific interests.

12. **Can this group continue as an ongoing small group after this course is over?** Yes. In the last session, the group is encouraged to make a contract or covenant to stay together and move on to the Growth Stage of a small group. A full description of the ongoing 201 Study courses are described inside the back cover.

13. **Are there other felt need courses available?** Yes, see page 61 for a complete list. For other curriculum for small groups, please call Serendipity at 1-800-525-9563.

CHECKLIST BEFORE THE SESSION

- ❏ ROOM ARRANGEMENT: Movable chairs for subdividing into groups of 4 to 6.

- ❏ HANDOUTS: Every person needs a Handout or the course book for every session. Permission is given for you to photocopy the Handout. Remember, there are two sides to the Handout. You may also want to photocopy the Caring Time part of the session as well.

- ❏ SPLIT SESSIONS: If you want to divide a session because you do not have 90 minutes, there is an Ice-Breaker to kick off the second part which you will need to photocopy from this book and give to the group.

- ❏ BIBLES: The Bible passage for discussion has been included in the Handout. However, if you want the group to read from their own Bibles, ask the people in the group to bring their Bibles.

- ❏ COURSE BOOK: Be sure to bring the book to the session and follow the agenda for each part of the session.

Agenda for Each Session

15 Minutes | **ICE-BREAKER / Groups of 4 to 6**
Divide the group into subgroups of 4 to 6 for a few minutes to get acquainted. Give the Handout—Side One to everyone.

You have permission to photocopy the Handout (both sides) for the session as needed, or you may prefer to provide each group member with his or her own course book.

5 Minutes | **INTRODUCTION TO THE ISSUE / All Together**
Bring the subgroups back together to listen to the introductory remarks for the session.

20 Minutes | **DISCUSS THE ISSUE / Groups of 4 to 6**
Regather in groups of 4 to 6 (same groups) to answer the questions on the Handout (Side One).

20 Minutes | **BIBLE STUDY / Same Groups of 4 to 6**
Stay in the same subgroups of 4 to 6 to discuss the Bible Study questions found on Side Two of the Handout.

Option 1: If you have a full 90 minutes for a session, follow the three-part agenda.

Option 2: If you only have 60 minutes for the session, do the Bible Study at the next session. A separate Ice-Breaker is provided for this Bible Study—which you will need to photocopy for group members.

20–30 Minutes | **CARING TIME / Same Groups of 4 to 6**
This is the most important part of every meeting. It is a time for sharing prayer requests and praying for one another. Be sure to stay with the agenda so that the Caring Time is not neglected.

SESSION 1

The Many Faces of Stress

OBJECTIVES

To begin to get to know each other, and to explore our own unique experience of stress.

To learn what stress is, and to discover the various life experiences which trigger a stress reaction.

To look at how Job experienced and responded to stress.

THREE-PART AGENDA

ICE-BREAKER
15 Minutes

ISSUE / BIBLE STUDY
45 Minutes

CARING TIME
30 Minutes

OPTION: If you only have 60 minutes, divide this session into two sessions, with the Bible Study section for your next time together.

ICE-BREAKER

Pass out the Handout for this session or the course book to each person. Divide the group into subgroups of 4 to 6 to get acquainted by doing the Ice-Breaker. (Photocopy pages 9 and 11 as needed.)

Go around the group on the first question. If you have time left, go around on the next question, etc.

1. Share your name and what you would probably be doing if you had not come to this group today.

2. Complete this sentence: "When I was in high school my friends would have described me as ... ." What were some things you did which made them see you this way?

3. How did you hear about this group, and what made you decide to come?

INTRODUCTION TO THE ISSUE

LEADER:

• Summarize these remarks (in your own words) into a brief introduction (no longer than 5 minutes).

• Be careful not to read the entire presentation to the group.

• In your presentation cover the "Discuss the Issue" questions listed on Side One of the Handout.

"I've got to get rid of the stress in my life!" How many times have you heard someone say that? Perhaps you have said it yourself. In our complex world, stress seems overwhelming at times. However, before you try to eliminate stress altogether, you should consider these words from Hans Selye, a researcher in the area of stress and stress management: "Complete freedom from stress is death."[1]

It's true! Stress is a natural response to change. We will be free of it only when we die (provided, of course, we won't have to make major adjustments in the afterlife!) Ironically, we can experience a great deal of stress just by expecting that life should not be stressful! The truth is, stress is not only part of life, but will enhance life if it is under control. It's like author Leo Buscaglia writes:

> "Don't ever believe that you are going to be peaceful—life is not like that. When you are changing all the time, you've got to keep adjusting to change, which means that you are going to be constantly facing new obstacles. That's the joy of living. And once you are involved in the process of becoming, there is no stopping. You're doomed! You're gone! But what a fantastic journey!"[2]

What we need to do, then, is not eliminate stress, but understand and manage it. We need to handle stress in such a way that it adds to life rather than destroys it. To do this we must understand what stress is. Stress is not anxiety or worry. These may add to stress, but stress is different. Neither does stress mean "pressure put on a person from his or her life." The same event may be experienced by one person as stressful and another person as nonstressful.

Stress is the reaction of a person's body to readjust or adapt in the light of the changes which come to life. These changes may be:

- **external**—problems at work, illness, death of a loved one, etc., or
- **internal**—new ideas or perceptions which call into question old values

Selye points out that both pleasant *and* unpleasant changes can cause stress. "All that counts," he says, is "the intensity of the demand" on us to readjust or adapt.[3] Being promoted at work, graduating from college, or getting married can all be quite stressful, even though we usually welcome all three events! Certainly we don't want to avoid pleasant situations just because they might be stressful. But we need to realize that even in the midst of good times, we will need to know how to manage stress.

There are many different sources of stress in life. Most fall under one of the following categories:

- **Financial stress**—Rachel, a single parent of two young girls, is living from day to day trying to make ends meet. Tom and Mary are up to their necks in debt and the bank is threatening to foreclose on their mortgage.

- **Relational stress**—Whatever spark there was in their marriage is gone now for Dan and Jessica. They never touch each other, and live with the constant expectation that the other person is angry with them.
- **Vocational stress**—Ed is a middle manager of a company which was recently acquired by a large corporation. Layoffs are expected within two months, and Ed has not hit it off with the new management. He is expecting he will lose his job.
- **Stress from life change**—Carol's mother died two months ago, and now her husband Roger has been diagnosed with prostate cancer.
- **Spiritual stress**—Ever since she filed for divorce, Cindy has felt guilty about disappointing her family and friends. God seems especially far away to her.

While it is helpful to separate these areas of stress, we should also remember that stress often arises in several areas at the same time. For instance, Ron moved to a new job in a new city (life change) because he was not being given the opportunity to grow in his skills as an engineer (vocational). Ron's stress was heightened when his house in the old city did not sell and the two mortgage payments per month nearly caused him to go bankrupt (financial). He was gruff and irritable with his family (relational), and his anger at God resulted in one extended period in which he was not able to even say grace at meal time (spiritual). While financial stress was perhaps central in Ron's situation, all other areas played a contributing role.

Taking charge
Since stress can come at us from several directions, it can at times seem overwhelming. The key is to focus on the inner attitudes and resources we use to deal with stress. No matter what the source of stress is, our attitudes make the difference between manageable and excessive stress.

It's like a story that minister and author John Claypool tells about his college days. He was alone in his dorm because everyone else had gone home on break. He was a little nervous being in a big dorm alone. Then, about two o'clock in the morning he heard a loud knock on his door. He imagined all kinds of things, including kidnappers coming for him! He even thought of jumping from the window (on the third floor!) to escape the imagined terrors on the other side of the door. Finally, he decided to just open the door and face it. He found a friend from the dorm who had returned early from break. He had just locked himself out of his room and was wanting a place to stay! Claypool wrote of his experience: "The terror I had experienced from the moment I awakened until I finally opened the door was entirely of my own making. It was what I had done to an event rather than what an event had done to me."[4]

The key to change is not in changing what is "out there," but what is inside of us. That means the key to change is in our own hands! In the sessions to come we will learn how to use that key.

SESSION ONE HANDOUT: Stress Management

The Many Faces of Stress

 ICE-BREAKER / Groups of 4 to 6 / 15 Minutes

Go around the group on the first question. If you have time left, go around on the next question, etc.

1. Share your name and what you would probably be doing if you had not come to this group today.

2. Complete this sentence: "When I was in high school my friends would have described me as ... ." What were some things you did which made them see you this way?

3. How did you hear about this group, and what made you decide to come?

 DISCUSS THE ISSUE / Same Groups / 20 Minutes
After a brief introduction by the leader, take turns sharing your responses to the following questions.

1. What stressful event do you remember your family going through when you were a child? What did your parent(s) do to manage that stress?

2. In reviewing the areas of life where we experience stress, which area do you find to be most common for people of your generation? Number them 1–5, with 1 being the most common and 5 being the least common.
   _____ financial stress   _____ stress from life change
   _____ relational stress   _____ spiritual stress
   _____ vocational stress

3. How would you rank the five areas above in your own life?

4. Which of the following physical signs of stress have you noticed in yourself recently?
   ❏ headaches   ❏ frequent colds   ❏ stomach problems
   ❏ heart palpitations ❏ muscle spasms   ❏ physical exhaustion
   ❏ insomnia   ❏ rashes / canker sores ❏ other:_____

5. How do you react to the idea that you hold the key to handling stress in your life?

6. What do you hope to receive from this group?
   ❏ the key to peace and happiness
   ❏ a chance to be with people wrestling with the same issues
   ❏ a listening ear
   ❏ a group to support me in doing things I already know I should be doing
   ❏ some ideas regarding strategies to manage my life
   ❏ a place to get some things off my chest

INTRODUCTION TO THE BIBLE STUDY

The story of Job, perhaps the oldest in the Bible, is proof that stress is nothing new. Most of Job's stress in this story comes from a specific kind of life change—a series of losses. Yet the kind of stress he felt was similar to what we feel when facing several sources of stress at the same time.

Job was a devout believer in God and had fared quite well in life. He had seven sons and three daughters. Such a large family was viewed as an indication of God's favor because one needed a large family in a farming culture to help with the work. The size of his herd also indicates that Job was a wealthy man. Job had 7,000 sheep, 3,000 camels, 500 yoke of oxen and 500 donkeys.

Job's fortune did not last, however. Scripture tells us that Satan was allowed to test Job (to find out what he was really made of) by a series of stressful life changes. Job's reaction to this stress is one of the great stories of all time.

ICE-BREAKER FOR TWO-SESSION OPTION
If you are doing the Bible Study as a separate session, start off this session by dividing this group into subgroups of 4 to 6 and answering the following questions. Photocopy and give this to the group.

---

1. If you could be a child again and have your parent(s) read you a story, which story would you choose?
   ❐ *The Little Engine That Could*
   ❐ *Cinderella*
   ❐ *Pinocchio*
   ❐ *The Velveteen Rabbit*
   ❐ *The Cat in the Hat*
   ❐ *Little Red Riding Hood*
   ❐ *Alice in Wonderland*
   ❐ *The Wizard of Oz*
   ❐ *Jack and the Beanstalk*
   ❐ other:_____

   What's your favorite part of the story?

2. What gave you the greatest pleasure when you were between 7 and 10 years old?

3. What do you do now that makes you feel like a kid again?

SESSION ONE BIBLE STUDY

> ¹³One day when Job's sons and daughters were feasting and drinking wine at the oldest brother's house, ¹⁴a messenger came to Job and said, "The oxen were plowing and the donkeys were grazing nearby, ¹⁵and the Sabeans attacked and carried them off. They put the servants to the sword, and I am the only one who has escaped to tell you!"
>
> ¹⁶While he was still speaking, another messenger came and said, "The fire of God fell from the sky and burned up the sheep and the servants, and I am the only one who has escaped to tell you!"
>
> ¹⁷While he was still speaking, another messenger came and said, "The Chaldeans formed three raiding parties and swept down on your camels and carried them off. They put the servants to the sword, and I am the only one who has escaped to tell you!"
>
> ¹⁸While he was still speaking, yet another messenger came and said, "Your sons and daughters were feasting and drinking wine at the oldest brother's house, ¹⁹when suddenly a mighty wind swept in from the desert and struck the four corners of the house. It collapsed on them and they are dead, and I am the only one who has escaped to tell you!"
>
> ²⁰At this, Job got up and tore his robe and shaved his head. Then he fell to the ground in worship ²¹and said:
>
> > "Naked I came from my mother's womb,
> > and naked I will depart.
> > The LORD gave and the LORD has taken away;
> > may the name of the LORD be praised."
>
> ²²In all this, Job did not sin by charging God with wrongdoing.
>
> *Job 1:13–22*

1. Had you been Job, how would you have reacted to this series of stressful losses?
   - ❏ If any more messengers come, I'm not home!
   - ❏ I must have done something to make God really mad.
   - ❏ There is no God!
   - ❏ I am an incompetent manager and parent; I couldn't protect what I had.
   - ❏ Why are others so lucky, and I'm so unlucky?
   - ❏ Like Job did—"The LORD gave and the LORD has taken away ..."
   - ❏ If all can be lost so quickly, I can't attach myself to anything or anyone!
   - ❏ "Naked I came from my mother's womb ..." (Job's response).

2. How could Job make such a strong statement of faith after so many tragic losses?
   - ❏ It hadn't really sunk in what had happened to him.
   - ❏ He thought if he were faithful, God would give everything back.
   - ❏ It was ingrained in him from a lifetime of faith-training.
   - ❏ He had nowhere else to turn but to God.
   - ❏ It shows this is just fiction—no real person would respond that way!

3. Describe a time in your life when, like Job, you experienced a series of stressful events, one right after the other, with little time to adjust in between.

OPTIONAL KICK-OFF QUIZ FOR FIRST SESSION

The following "Life Events Survey" was developed by Dr. Thomas Holmes and Dr. Richard Rahe to measure stress from life changes. Each event on the list has a value in "Life Change Units" (LCUs), which is listed across from the event. Go through the list and mark each event which has occurred in your life in the last two years. Multiply the number of occurrences of that event times the "mean value" in LCUs. Then add the scores for all the events for your total LCU score. If you have an LCU Score of 300 or more, you are in danger of developing a disease related to stress.[5]

		Number Of Occurrences	Mean Value	Total
1.	death of a spouse	___	100	___
2.	divorce	___	73	___
3.	marital separation	___	65	___
4.	jail term	___	63	___
5.	death of a close family member	___	63	___
6.	personal injury or illness	___	53	___
7.	getting married	___	50	___
8.	fired at work	___	47	___
9.	marital reconciliation	___	45	___
10.	retirement	___	45	___
11.	change in health of family member	___	44	___
12.	pregnancy (both spouses affected)	___	40	___
13.	sexual difficulties	___	39	___
14.	gain of a new family member	___	39	___
15.	change in financial state	___	38	___
16.	death of a close friend	___	37	___
17.	change to a different line of work	___	36	___
18.	change in number of arguments with spouse	___	35	___
19.	mortgage / loan over $10,000	___	31	___
20.	foreclosure of mortgage or loan	___	30	___
21.	change in responsibilities at work	___	29	___
22.	son or daughter leaving home	___	29	___
23.	trouble with in-laws	___	29	___
24.	outstanding personal achievement	___	28	___
25.	spouse began or stopped work	___	26	___
26.	began or ended school	___	26	___
27.	change in living conditions	___	25	___
28.	revision of personal habits	___	24	___
29.	trouble with boss	___	23	___
30.	change in work hours or conditions	___	20	___
31.	change in residence	___	20	___
32.	change in schools	___	20	___
33.	change in recreation	___	19	___
34.	change in church activities	___	19	___
35.	change in social activities	___	18	___
36.	mortgage/loan less than $10,000	___	17	___
37.	change in sleeping habits	___	16	___
38.	change in number of family get-togethers	___	15	___
39.	change in eating habits	___	15	___
40.	vacation	___	13	___
41.	Christmas	___	12	___
42.	minor violations of the law	___	11	___

TOTAL LCU Score ___

CARING TIME

Take time now to share any personal prayer requests. Start out by asking everyone to answer this question:

"How can we help you in prayer this week?"

Take turns praying for each other, remembering the requests that have been shared. If you would like to pray in silence, say the word "Amen" when you have finished your prayer, so that the next person will know when to start. At the close, join hands and repeat together the following promises of Scripture:

*So do not fear, for I am with you;
do not be dismayed, for I am your God.
I will strengthen you and help you;
I will uphold you with my righteous right hand.
(Isaiah 41:10)*

*"Come to me, all you who are weary and burdened,
and I will give you rest.
Take my yoke upon you and learn from me,
for I am gentle and humble in heart,
and you will find rest for your souls.
For my yoke is easy and my burden is light."
(Matthew 11:28-30)*

LEADER:

If applicable, have the group use the extra space on this page for group prayer requests.

SESSION 2

Setting Your Own Pace

OBJECTIVES

To discover how trying to please others adds to stress, often making it unmanageable.

To discover and share our own activity pace.

To see how even Jesus was pressured by others to live according to their pace, and to learn from how he handled that.

THREE-PART AGENDA

 **ICE-BREAKER**
15 Minutes

 **ISSUE / BIBLE STUDY**
45 Minutes

 **CARING TIME**
30 Minutes

OPTION: If you only have 60 minutes, divide this session into two sessions, with the Bible Study section for your next time together.

ICE-BREAKER

Pass out the Handout for this session or the course book to each person. Divide the group into subgroups of 4 to 6 to get acquainted by doing the Ice-Breaker. (Photocopy pages 17 and 19 as needed.)

1. In your workplace, what motivates you most to get a job done?
   - ❏ fear of getting fired
   - ❏ deadlines
   - ❏ competition
   - ❏ being trusted
   - ❏ pride
   - ❏ making money
   - ❏ teamwork
   - ❏ other:_____

2. What is one job you try to get done as quickly as you can?

3. What is one job you like to take your time doing?

INTRODUCTION TO THE ISSUE

LEADER:

• Summarize these remarks (in your own words) into a brief introduction (no longer than 5 minutes).

• Be careful not to read the entire presentation to the group.

• In your presentation cover the "Discuss the Issue" questions listed on Side One of the Handout.

Author Bruce Larson tells the story of a little girl he met once who was trying to get her grandfather's attention at a swimming pool. She wanted him to pay attention to all of the wonderful things she could do, but he was busily engaged in conversation and was unaware of her efforts. Larson asked the little girl to show him. This she consented to grudgingly, and took a quick dive and swam across the pool. But as she climbed out of the pool, she resumed her previous efforts, crying "Granddaddy! Granddaddy! Come see what I can do!"[6] Apparently, it didn't matter at all to her that Bruce Larson watched what she could do. He was not her "audience of significance."

Even as adults, many of us are still saying, "See what I can do! See what I can do!" to a parent, spouse or other person who is important to us. Usually it is a parent or grandparent, but sometimes it's people in general. As minister and author John Claypool writes, "We have an audience which is not God at all—not even in our religious actions—but a group of other human beings whose approval we crave at any cost."[7] Unfortunately, we never impress this audience as much as we need to, so we try harder. The result is an excess of stress in our life.

To manage stress, then, we have to set our own pace. This means essentially three things:

- not wasting energy trying to prove our worth or goodness,
- setting our own priorities for our life, and
- finding our balance between activity and rest.

Accepting our worth

Trying to prove our worth or goodness to others uses a tremendous amount of energy. We do things we otherwise wouldn't do, things we think are going to impress people.

Mark

Mark was one who tried hard to be seen by everyone as a "nice guy." He tried to do anything anyone asked of him, especially at his church. When the minister resigned, he began doing much of what the minister had been doing until a new minister could be found. He began to get angry, however, because nobody appreciated him the way he thought he deserved. Since he wanted people to think of him as a "nice guy," he repressed his anger and just kept trying to impress people. When the new minister came he turned to community work, eventually running for office. But again, people didn't appreciate his efforts as much as Mark thought they should. So he tried to do more. In the midst of all this, Mark had a heart attack at age 39. While Mark was overweight and was having some financial difficulties, it is quite possible that it was his effort to prove himself that pushed his stress level beyond his ability to manage it.

We need to accept our worth as a given instead of trying to prove we deserve it. The basis of our worth is that each person has been made in the image of God. Christians lay claim to an additional source of value as God's children and heirs (Gal. 4:6–7). Since God declares we have worth, we do not need to prove it to others.

Setting priorities for life
Setting our own pace also means setting some priorities. Other people have their priorities for us: the boss wants us to put work first; the church wants us to give ministry priority time; any clubs or organizations we belong to make their demands; and our family lays claims on our "prime time." What is most important? If we try to do what everyone else wants us to do, we will be run ragged. That can even happen if we just do all of the things we would "like" to do. Only when we set priorities ourselves will we get stress under control.

Richard
Richard was a recovering alcoholic who was trying to reestablish himself in his career as a graphic designer. At the same time, he was taking on the parenting responsibilities of his two girls, ages 8 and 16. He wanted to spend a lot of time with his girls to build a relationship with them. However, his previous problems with alcohol had brought many debts, and in order to get out from under that debt in the time he wanted to he needed to work overtime. In addition, Alcoholics Anonymous and his church were making demands on his time. He also wanted to spend some free time doing noncommercial art. With all these demands, Richard found very little time for his girls, no time for his art, and a growing frustration with life.

Richard's excess stress came from trying to do too much too quickly, without setting priorities.

Balancing between activity and rest
After we have set our priorities we still need to determine how much we can do toward reaching them. Some people function well when they are always busy, while others must have ample periods of quiet recovery time between tasks. Hans Selye writes:

> The average citizen would suffer just as much from the boredom of purposeless subsistence as from the inevitable fatigue created by the constant pursuit of perfection: in other words, the majority equally dislike a lack of stress and an excess of it. Hence each of us must carefully analyze himself and try to find the particular stress level at which he feels most comfortable. ...[8]

In a long-distance race, each runner must decide his own pacing—whether to hold back and try to come on strong at the end, or run as fast as possible for the entire race. Either strategy can win the race, but only if the runner holds to his or her own strategy. Those who try to run someone else's race will lose. That is true with life, too! Only when we set our own pace will we live our life in the most effective way.

SESSION TWO HANDOUT: Stress Management

Setting Your Own Pace

ICE-BREAKER / Groups of 4 to 6 / 15 Minutes

1. In your workplace, what motivates you most to get a job done?
   - ❑ fear of getting fired
   - ❑ making money
   - ❑ being trusted
   - ❑ pride
   - ❑ competition
   - ❑ deadlines
   - ❑ teamwork
   - ❑ other:_____

2. What is one job you try to get done as quickly as you can?

3. What is one job you like to take your time doing?

DISCUSS THE ISSUE / Same Groups / 20 Minutes
After a brief introduction by the leader, take turns sharing your responses to the following questions.

1. In your life, who do you find yourself still trying to impress?
   - ❑ my mother
   - ❑ my father
   - ❑ my boss
   - ❑ God
   - ❑ my spouse
   - ❑ a grandparent
   - ❑ people in general
   - ❑ a brother or sister
   - ❑ an adult mentor
   - ❑ other:_____

2. Choose from the following areas to make your ideal priority list. Then make another list that shows the order of your actual priorities in life. (Rank them 1–10.)

PRIORITIES	IDEAL	ACTUAL
my spouse or "significant other"	_____	_____
my children	_____	_____
my job / providing financially	_____	_____
my church	_____	_____
the less fortunate	_____	_____
my private time	_____	_____
community activities	_____	_____
my friends	_____	_____
my extended family	_____	_____
fitness activities	_____	_____

3. Which of the following do you need to do to reduce stress in your life?
   - ❑ accept my worth and stop living my life for someone else
   - ❑ reorder my life according to my own priorities
   - ❑ figure out what my priorities really are
   - ❑ reduce my activity level to a more peaceful pace
   - ❑ increase my activity level to alleviate stressful boredom

INTRODUCTION TO THE BIBLE STUDY

The events in this passage are described by Mark as occurring very early in Jesus' ministry. Jesus had just called the first of his disciples, then had gone to Capernaum, not far from his hometown of Nazareth.

Sometimes we are led to believe that Jesus' ministry was without stress until the last few weeks, when he had to face his arrest and death. "After all," we say, "he was popular and everyone hung on his every word. People invited him into their homes, to banquets and wedding feasts. What's so difficult about that?" This passage, however, presents a different story. Here we see a man who was under tremendous pressure to perform and conform. That Jesus experienced this pressure shows that Jesus knows how we feel. As the book of Hebrews says, "We do not have a high priest who is unable to sympathize with our weaknesses ..." (Heb. 4:15).

> **ICE-BREAKER FOR TWO-SESSION OPTION**
> *If you are doing the Bible Study as a separate session, start off this session by dividing this group into subgroups of 4 to 6 and answering the following questions. Photocopy and give this to the group.*

1. The phone rings at dinner time and a charitable organization is calling to ask for a donation? What do you do?
   ❒ ask them to call back in an hour
   ❒ say, "No thanks"
   ❒ say, "Yes"
   ❒ hang up
   ❒ criticize them for calling at dinner time and then hang up
   ❒ tell them we don't respond to requests over the phone
   ❒ other:_____

2. When someone you know asks for your help and says, "It will only take a minute," what thoughts go through your mind?

SESSION TWO BIBLE STUDY

³⁵Very early in the morning, while it was still dark, Jesus got up, left the house and went off to a solitary place, where he prayed. ³⁶Simon and his companions went to look for him, ³⁷and when they found him, they exclaimed, "Everyone is looking for you!"

³⁸Jesus replied, "Let us go somewhere else—to the nearby villages—so I can preach there also. That is why I have come." ³⁹So he traveled throughout Galilee, preaching in their synagogues and driving out demons.

⁴⁰A man with leprosy came to him and begged him on his knees, "If you are willing, you can make me clean."

⁴¹Filled with compassion, Jesus reached out his hand and touched the man. "I am willing," he said. "Be clean!" ⁴²Immediately his leprosy left him and he was cured.

⁴³Jesus sent him away at once with a strong warning: ⁴⁴"See that you don't tell this to anyone. But go, show yourself to the priest and offer the sacrifices that Moses commanded for your cleansing, as a testimony to them. ⁴⁵Instead he went out and began to talk freely, spreading the news. As a result, Jesus could no longer enter a town openly but stayed outside in lonely places. Yet the people still came to him from everywhere.

Mark 1:35–45

1. If you had been alone having a private prayer time and the disciples came looking for you, how would you have felt?
   - ❒ angry that I couldn't have even one minute alone
   - ❒ like telling the disciples to leave me alone so I could keep praying
   - ❒ like inviting the disciples to pray with me
   - ❒ like postponing prayer and doing what was most needed at the time
   - ❒ gratified that I was so needed
   - ❒ guilty that I wasn't around when needed
   - ❒ torn between my need to be alone and my desire to help others
   - ❒ other:_____

2. Which of the things Jesus faced cause you the most stress?
   - ❒ short nights (v. 35)
   - ❒ always on the go (v. 39)
   - ❒ having routines disrupted (v. 37)
   - ❒ being physically crowded (v. 45)
   - ❒ constant demands (vv. 37,40,45)
   - ❒ people not respecting my wishes (vv. 43–45a)

3. Where do you go, and what do you do, when you need some time alone? How often do you make such time for yourself?

4. When has there been a time when you felt like there was no place you could go to escape the demands on you? What did you do?

5. What is the most stressful or difficult thing in your life right now? What difference could getting alone to pray make in handling that situation?

REFERENCE NOTES

Mark 1:35–45

1:35 *he prayed.* In the midst of great success, Jesus is quick to acknowledge his dependence on God as the source of his power.

1:36–37 In contrast to Jesus, who sought the Father's will, Simon Peter and the other disciples were simply following the will of the people. It seemed natural to them to remain where Jesus was so appreciated.

1:38 *so I can preach there also.* Jesus' ministry was not primarily to be one of healing and exorcism. Rather, these were signs of what his message of God's kingdom was all about. He refuses to be sidetracked by popular demand. He knows what his life is all about—proclaiming ("preaching") the kingdom of God (see vv. 14–15).

1:40 *leprosy.* No disease was dreaded more than leprosy, since it brought not only physical disfigurement but social banishment.

came to him. What the leper did was forbidden by Jewish religious law.

If you are willing. The leper had no doubt about Jesus' ability. However, since leprosy was considered a sign of God's judgment against a person because of sin, the man was uncertain of Jesus' willingness.

1:41 *Filled with compassion.* Human suffering evoked a deep, emotional response from Jesus.

touched. Actually touching a leper was unimaginable to most first-century people. Not only did one risk contracting the disease, but such contact made the well person ritually impure, and thus unable to participate in the religious life of the community. The effect of Jesus' touch on this leper must have been overwhelming.

1:43 *don't tell this to anyone.* Jesus realized that this miracle would draw even greater crowds of people wanting to be healed, and that this would restrict his opportunities to preach. It was an impossible command to obey, however, and the man ignored it! The result was more pressure on Jesus.

as a testimony to them. Under the Old Testament Law, only a priest could pronounce whether or not a person suspected of having leprosy was actually cured (Lev. 14:1–32). Such certification was vital to a leper: it was that person's way back into normal contact with human society. If a priest declared this man clean, he would in effect be bearing witness to the religious establishment that Jesus indeed had power to heal a disease which, in the Old Testament, only Moses and the great prophet Elijah ever had been able to heal. This would be an indication of Jesus' exalted status.

CARING TIME

Remember that this time is for developing and expressing your caring for each other as group members. You can do this by sharing any personal prayer requests and praying for each other's needs. Start by answering the question:

"How do you need God's help in balancing your life and setting priorities?"

Then share any other prayer requests and take turns praying for each other. Close by thanking God for bringing you together as a group and asking him to help you grow through the stress and difficulties of life.

LEADER:

If applicable, have the group use the extra space on this page for group prayer requests.

SESSION 3

Listening to Body Language

OBJECTIVES

To show how physical self-care, in the form of diet, rest and exercise, is an important part of stress management.

To see how physical ailments can result from mismanaged stress.

To consider some biblical views on the importance of the body and its care.

THREE-PART AGENDA

ICE-BREAKER
15 Minutes

ISSUE / BIBLE STUDY
45 Minutes

CARING TIME
30 Minutes

OPTION: If you only have 60 minutes, divide this session into two sessions, with the Bible Study section for your next time together.

ICE-BREAKER

Pass out the Handout for this session or the course book to each person. Divide the group into subgroups of 4 to 6 to do the Ice-Breaker. (Photocopy pages 25 and 27 as needed.)

1. At what age were you in the best shape of your life physically? What were you doing for exercise?

2. Which of the following would be the most upsetting order your doctor could give you?
   ❏ Eat less than 1,000 calories a day.
   ❏ Walk two miles a day.
   ❏ Do 50 sit-ups and push-ups a day.
   ❏ Ride an exercise bike 30 minutes a day.
   ❏ Join an aerobics class.
   ❏ Give up smoking / alcohol.
   ❏ Cut out all sweets.
   ❏ Stop playing _____.
   ❏ Take six months off from work.
   ❏ Take a vacation.
   ❏ Start attending church.
   ❏ See a counselor.

INTRODUCTION TO THE ISSUE

LEADER:

• Summarize these remarks (in your own words) into a brief introduction (no longer than 5 minutes).

• Be careful not to read the entire presentation to the group.

• In your presentation cover the "Discuss the Issue" questions listed on Side One of the Handout.

"No pain, no gain!"—that's what the exercise gurus used to preach. If you wanted real benefit from exercise, you had to ignore those pain signals and push past them to "feel the burn." Track coaches exalted the runner who pushed to the finish, ignoring the pain of cramping muscles. Some athletic coaches still teach such an approach, but many in the field of physical fitness are seeing things from a different perspective today. Exercise does not have to be painful. In fact, ignoring pain can lead to injury or even death. When it comes to fitness, the wise person listens to his or her body.

The physical impact of stress

Some of us deal with the stress of living in the same way that these old fitness gurus did. We ignore the pain and we push on toward our goal. Life becomes a long-distance race where the winners are the ones who "gut it out" to the end. No wonder that heart disease is our #1 killer!

Physicians and scientists who study stress tell us we cannot ignore what our body says to us. Every episode of mismanaged stress is registered in our body like a bank debit. And as with a bank account, you can only have so many debits before you drain your account. Stress researcher Hans Selye writes: "Each period of stress, especially if it results from frustrating, unsuccessful struggles, leaves some irreversible chemical scars which accumulate to constitute the signs of aging."[9]

The importance of regular exercise

A regular program of exercise is an essential part of a program of stress management.

Selye differentiates between *stress* and *distress.* Stress is something we should not try to avoid because it is a natural and healthy part of life. Distress is mismanaged stress, and leads to health problems. Selye writes: "Certain emotional factors, such as frustration, are particularly likely to turn stress into distress, whereas in most instances, physical exercise has the opposite effect."[10]

Exercise releases adrenaline, a natural antidepressant, into the blood stream. It also refocuses energy from abstract problems (with a high frustration level) to a concrete diversion. With exercise, we can accomplish a specific task in a relatively short period of time.

Ken

Ken found that exercise helped him more than anything else during his times of financial stress. His bills were coming in regularly at the rate of $200 a month more than the family income, and he was seeing nowhere to trim. His frustration was leading to regular arguments with his wife. This upset him because, although they differed in spending philosophy, she really wasn't to blame for the dilemma either. What really was surprising was that there didn't seem to be anything Ken could do to change the situation. Prayer helped, but he found his mind going quickly back to finances and his frustration level would rise again. When he started running at night, however, he found that it released much of the tension that had been building up in his body. The combination of prayer followed by exercise seemed to help most of all.

The importance of having a proper diet

Vitamins and minerals are an important part of the body's way of storing extra energy we need in times of stress. When we don't get a well-rounded diet, our body is less prepared to weather such times. Unfortunately, when we're under a lot of stress, we often eat "on the run," and what we eat is "fast food," which lacks the nutritional balance we need.

The need for adequate rest

Rest renews the spirit as well as the body. Problems which seem absolutely overwhelming at night may appear much more manageable in the morning. That's because the body has more energy to handle stress after a good night of rest. It is also true, however, that when stress becomes excessive to the point of depression, some people sleep to escape reality. In such situations no amount of rest is ever adequate. Clinical psychologist Martin Shaffer writes:

> As people sink deeper into the stage of exhaustion, their behavior appears more and more like depression: They experience fatigue that, typically, is not alleviated by sleep, and feel a vague sense of anxiety. They become apathetic and humorless—and withdraw even further into sleep, television or fantasy.[11]

While sleeping too much is a problem for some, more people who are mismanaging stress have just the opposite problem: They cannot get the sleep they need to stay healthy. Most adults need about eight hours of sleep. If you are sleeping significantly less (or more) than that, you should probably make an appointment to see your doctor.

The importance of having a varied activity schedule

Hans Selye writes that one of the biggest contributors to stress is frustration. There is a way of handling the stress that comes from frustration, however. Selye writes: "In stress research, we have found that, when completion of one particular task becomes impossible, diversion, a voluntary change of activity, is frequently as good as—if not better than—a rest."[12]

For instance, Peter, who writes professionally, finds that when he gets "writer's block," it helps him to work in his garden for a while. He finds the task of pulling weeds much better than rest for relieving his stress.

None of the four elements we have discussed (exercise, diet, rest and varied activities) is a cure-all for stress in itself. But taken together they contribute to a balanced physical approach to stress management. When we really listen, we learn it is just this balanced approach our bodies are longing for.

SESSION THREE HANDOUT: Stress Management

Listening to Body Language

 ICE-BREAKER / Groups of 4 to 6 / 15 Minutes

1. At what age were you in the best shape of your life physically? What were you doing for exercise?

2. Which of the following would be the most upsetting order your doctor could give you?
   - ❏ Eat less than 1,000 calories a day.
   - ❏ Do 50 sit-ups and push-ups a day.
   - ❏ Ride an exercise bike 30 minutes a day.
   - ❏ Give up smoking / alcohol.
   - ❏ Stop playing _____.
   - ❏ Take a vacation.
   - ❏ Walk two miles a day.
   - ❏ Join an aerobics class.
   - ❏ See a counselor.
   - ❏ Cut out all sweets.
   - ❏ Take six months off from work.
   - ❏ Start attending church.

DISCUSS THE ISSUE / Same Groups / 20 Minutes
After a brief introduction by the leader, take turns sharing your responses to the following questions.

1. When you are experiencing a lot of frustration with a task, do you find it more helpful to rest or switch to another activity? What activity do you prefer as a diversion?

2. In each of the following areas, rate yourself from 1 to 10 on how well you are doing (place an *"X"* on the lines below).

   EXERCISE
   ```
   1      2      3      4      5      6      7      8      9      10
   No discipline         Moderate discipline              High discipline
   ```

   DIET
   ```
   1      2      3      4      5      6      7      8      9      10
   No discipline         Moderate discipline              High discipline
   ```

   REST
   ```
   1      2      3      4      5      6      7      8      9      10
   No discipline         Moderate discipline              High discipline
   ```

   VARIED ACTIVITIES
   ```
   1      2      3      4      5      6      7      8      9      10
   No discipline         Moderate discipline              High discipline
   ```

3. If your body could talk, what would your body say to you right now?
   - ❏ "Slow down!"
   - ❏ "Feed me—right!"
   - ❏ "Shape up (exercise) or I'm going to ship out!"
   - ❏ "Take a break!"
   - ❏ "Get some rest!"
   - ❏ "Just say no (to_____)!"

INTRODUCTION TO THE BIBLE STUDY

The Bible has a lot to say about the way you physically treat yourself! Two passages, in particular, show how God views us. From these words, we learn something about how we should take care of ourselves.

The first passage is from Psalm 139. The primary purpose of this psalm is to praise God for his complete knowledge of the writer (and of all of us). God knows our past and future. He knows our every motivation and thought, no matter where we are. And he knows our bodies—the inner workings of who we are. In exalting God this passage also, in effect, declares the human body as one of God's greatest works. The second passage is from a letter Paul wrote to the Corinthian church regarding sexual immorality on the part of some of the members. Evidently some in the church were convinced by a prominent Greek idea that the physical and spiritual are so different that what a person does with the physical body has no effect on them spiritually. Such an idea is not only wrong in terms of sexual behavior, but also in terms of the way we treat the physical body in general. If the body is the Holy Spirit's temple, as Paul here declares, then everything we do to that body has spiritual implications.

> **ICE-BREAKER FOR TWO-SESSION OPTION**
> *If you are doing the Bible Study as a separate session, start off this session by dividing this group into subgroups of 4 to 6 and answering the following questions. Photocopy and give this to the group.*

Have one person at a time complete all three of the following sentences concerning their "dream vacation."

1. For my dream vacation I would go to:
   - ❏ Europe
   - ❏ the Rocky Mountains
   - ❏ Disney World
   - ❏ Australia
   - ❏ a ski resort in the Alps
   - ❏ Niagara Falls
   - ❏ Hawaii
   - ❏ the Virgin Islands
   - ❏ the Holy Land
   - ❏ Alaska
   - ❏ other:_____

2. I would take:
   - ❏ just my spouse
   - ❏ my best friend, _____
   - ❏ Tom Cruise
   - ❏ Julia Roberts
   - ❏ Richard Gere
   - ❏ Cindy Crawford
   - ❏ my parents
   - ❏ my whole family
   - ❏ a group of friends
   - ❏ nobody
   - ❏ other:_____

3. I would spend most of my time:
   - ❏ doing absolutely nothing
   - ❏ reading
   - ❏ fishing or hiking
   - ❏ skiing
   - ❏ touring the sights
   - ❏ on the beach
   - ❏ in romantic pursuits
   - ❏ other:_____

SESSION THREE BIBLE STUDY

¹³For you created my inmost being;
you knit me together in my mother's womb.
¹⁴I praise you because I am fearfully and wonderfully made;
your works are wonderful,
I know that full well.
¹⁵My frame was not hidden from you
when I was made in the secret place.
When I was woven together in the depths of the earth,
¹⁶   your eyes saw my unformed body.
All the days ordained for me
were written in your book
before one of them came to be.   Psalm 139:13–16

¹⁹Do you not know that your body is a temple of the Holy Spirit, who is in you, whom you have received from God? You are not your own; ²⁰you were bought at a price. Therefore honor God with your body.   1 Corinthians 6:19–20

1. Why do you think it is important to know that our bodies were not hidden from God when they were made, but rather God saw them even before they were formed?

2. What is the main implication for stress management of the fact that you are "fearfully and wonderfully made"?
   ❑ I'm tough—I can survive any abuse!
   ❑ I have a lot of resiliency—but I shouldn't abuse it.
   ❑ I should preserve the sacred artistry of what God made in me.
   ❑ other:_____

3. How does your attitude toward yourself affect the amount of stress in your life?
   ❑ Destroying my body is one way of getting back at myself.
   ❑ Destroying my body is one way of getting back at God.
   ❑ I keep thinking that if I just do enough, I will like myself.
   ❑ I expect a lot of myself, and that is stressful.
   ❑ I am happy with what I have done, and that relieves stress.

4. If you are to "honor God with your body," what do you most need to do?
   ❑ believe I am worth caring for
   ❑ develop more self-discipline
   ❑ realize it makes a difference to God how I care for my body
   ❑ appreciate the wonders of the body God has given me
   ❑ quit running around trying to honor people, and instead honor God
   ❑ stop polluting the one and only "natural resource" I've got
   ❑ become less influenced by the "ways of the world"

REFERENCE NOTES

Psalm 139:13–16

139:13 *you knit me together.* The psalmist, David, speaks of how he was "woven together" (v. 15), suggesting a metaphor of creating a tapestry of complex colors and patterns (Kidner).

139:14 The marvel of his own body leads the psalmist to worship God as his creator. How much more might modern people (far more aware than David ever could have been of the complexity of systems involved in the ability to see, taste, hear, smell, eat, breathe, reproduce, think, etc.) marvel at the Creator's power and wisdom.

139:15 The author ponders the mystery of his existence as an act of God's knowledge and power.

the depths of the earth. This is a metaphor for the womb.

139:16 *All the days ordained for me were written in your book.* This reflects the author's conviction that his total lifespan is fully known by God (v. 5). The notion that the Lord keeps a book on the lives of people is found many places in Scripture (including Psalm 69:28; Ex. 32:32–33; Dan. 12:1 and Mal. 3:16). That the days of the psalmist's life were outlined before he was alive was not a fatalistic idea. Rather, it was comforting to know that God completely knew him and controlled the circumstances of his life.

1 Corinthians 6:19–20

6:19 The temple was the sacred place where God dwelt with his people. The Jews took great care to treat the temple with respect and to teach children to do the same. In 1 Corinthians 3:10, Paul referred to the church as a structure that God was building. Here Paul refers to the body as the temple of the Holy Spirit. Should we not teach respect for these "temples" as much as we do a church building?

6:20 *bought at a price.* The image is of ransoming slaves from their bondage. In the same way, Christ has paid the ransom price to free Christians from the bondage of sin. They now belong to him. The way they use their bodies is to reflect this new loyalty.

CARING TIME

Begin by sharing any personal prayer requests and then answering the question:

"What would you like to change in the way you handle stress?"

Go around the group and have each person pray for the person on their right, remembering the concerns that have been shared. Start with this sentence:

"Dear God, I want to talk with you about my friend _____."

When each person has had a turn, join hands and thank God that he loves us more than we can know and promises to meet our every need.

LEADER:

If applicable, have the group use the extra space on this page for group prayer requests.

SESSION 4

Keeping Your Focus

OBJECTIVES

To understand why having a life purpose is essential to managing stress.

To realize the importance of focusing on the here and now.

To consider how Jesus' teaching about anxiety in Matthew 6:25–34 can help us manage stress.

THREE-PART AGENDA

ICE-BREAKER
15 Minutes

ISSUE / BIBLE STUDY
45 Minutes

CARING TIME
30 Minutes

OPTION: If you only have 60 minutes, divide this session into two sessions, with the Bible Study section for your next time together.

ICE-BREAKER

Pass out the Handout for this session or the course book to each person. Divide the group into subgroups of 4 to 6 to do the Ice-Breaker. (Photocopy pages 33 and 35 as needed.).

1. Who did you share your dreams about your future with when you were in sixth grade?
   ❏ my best friend   ❏ a teacher
   ❏ my parents   ❏ nobody—They would have laughed!
   ❏ my brother or sister   ❏ other:_____
   ❏ a grandparent

2. What dreams did you have about your future at that time?

3. Today, where do you place yourself on the following line?

   ```
   1     2     3     4     5     6     7     8     9     10
   Nose to the grindstone                       Head in the clouds
   ```

INTRODUCTION TO THE ISSUE

LEADER:

• Summarize these remarks (in your own words) into a brief introduction (no longer than 5 minutes).

• Be careful not to read the entire presentation to the group.

• In your presentation cover the "Discuss the Issue" questions listed on Side One of the Handout.

There may be no more basic questions in life than "Who am I?" "Why am I here?" and "Where am I going?" And our answers to these questions have a great deal to do with the way we handle stress!

Why? Because they give us our bearings. Like a ship crossing the ocean, we have no guarantee of smooth sailing. We need to be prepared to ride out the unexpected storms and, when they are over, to find our direction and get back on course. Our life purpose is like the North Star. The clearer we see it, the more likely we are to find our way toward fulfilling our hopes and dreams and to handle disappointment when it comes.

Discovering a life purpose

How do we discover our life purpose? The best clue is to measure what it is we give most of our time and energy to, and what it is that we think about before we go to sleep and as soon as we wake up. Our actions speak louder than words. We may say our purpose is "to glorify God" or "to love my family," but live as if our greatest desire is to gain personal peace and prosperity!

Consider these "purpose statements" focusing on God, self and country:

> "Love the Lord your God with all your heart and with all your soul and with all your mind and with all your strength. ... Love your neighbor as yourself." —Jesus

> "Know thyself." —Socrates

> "I only regret that I have but one life to give for my country." —Nathan Hale

Defining our purpose, objectives and goals

It is helpful to make a distinction between purpose, objectives and goals:

1. **Purpose**—In one overarching sentence or phrase, what is your life all about? This statement must be broad enough to hold true for each area of your life. Examples:
   • "To glorify God and enjoy him forever." (Westminster Catechism)
   • "To live life to the fullest and help others to do so."

2. **Objectives**—Consider the four or five main areas of your life and give a general statement of intention for each. Examples:
   • Job—Jim, a division manager, defines his objective this way: "To communicate the goals of the company and motivate employees to do their best work."
   • Marriage—John and Mary approach their marriage with the idea of finding ways "to honor and to cherish" one another in all they do.
   • Family—The Sanders' family rules are simple: Love, respect and help one another.

3. **Goals**—For each general objective, you need two or three specific goals. Goals can be measured and are often short-term. Examples:

- Job—Susan is working to complete a master's degree in business administration in order to qualify for a promotion in the future.
- Marriage—Nick aims to take his wife out on a date at least twice a month.
- Family—Ed aims to give each of his four children at least five minutes per day and an hour per week of his undivided attention.

Focusing on the here and now

Having a life purpose and identifying objectives and goals gives us an important perspective. But it does not make us "worry-free." We can (and must) limit the stress brought about by anxiety over tomorrow. We have four courses of action:

1. **Finding pleasure in the present**

    If we look for and find pleasure in what is happening today, then whether tomorrow goes as planned is not so crucial. We are not banking all our happiness on those plans. We are enjoying each moment as it is, not as we planned it to be. This is especially important if we have children.

2. **Dealing with today's conflicts now**

    Putting off unpleasant situations creates a backlog which makes the future more and more fearful. The key to facing a problem or conflict is to focus on a greater good that can come from such confrontation.[13]

3. **Dealing with the past**

    Failing to confront pains in our past can cause stress to continue. If we have not dealt with our anger toward an authoritarian parent, for instance, it can cause us stress when we're dealing with persons in authority. Some individuals need counseling to confront such past issues. However, many have found that a disciplined prayer life can help tremendously.

4. **Having a perspective of faith**

    When we can look at what is happening around us through the eyes of faith, we see the fearful things as temporary and ultimately under the control of God. But we also need to believe in our own ability to handle what comes our way, and to believe that our friends will be there for us when we need them.

A study of Green Berets in Vietnam found that these combat soldiers relied on three methods to fight anxiety: belief in self, belief in their leaders, and belief in God.[14] The same combination helps us defeat anxiety in noncombat situations.

Focusing on today, rather than worrying about tomorrow, takes more than a decision not to worry. It takes an awareness of today's pleasures, a willingness to confront the conflicts of today and the pain of yesterday, and a lifestyle of belief. This combination can keep today's stress limited to what we can handle today.

SESSION FOUR HANDOUT: Stress Management

Keeping Your Focus

ICE-BREAKER / Groups of 4 to 6 / 15 Minutes

1. Who did you share your dreams about your future with when you were in sixth grade?
   - ❏ my best friend
   - ❏ my parents
   - ❏ my brother or sister
   - ❏ a grandparent
   - ❏ a teacher
   - ❏ nobody—They would have laughed!
   - ❏ other:_____

2. What dreams did you have about your future at that time?

3. Today, where do you place yourself on the following line?

   1   2   3   4   5   6   7   8   9   10
   Nose to the grindstone   **Head in the clouds**

DISCUSS THE ISSUE / Same Groups / 20 Minutes
After a brief introduction by the leader, take turns sharing your responses to the following questions.

1. In which of these areas do you think most people experience the greatest stress on a daily basis?
   - ❏ Purpose—They're deeply confused about the big questions of life.
   - ❏ Objectives—Their marriage, family, job, church, community, etc. aren't all that they had hoped them to be.
   - ❏ Goals—They are bogged down with short-term projects and day-to-day living.

2. In which of the following ways of limiting stress do you feel strongest? Weakest?
   - ❏ finding pleasure in the present
   - ❏ dealing with today's conflicts now
   - ❏ dealing with past pain
   - ❏ believing in myself
   - ❏ believing in others
   - ❏ believing in God

3. How satisfying is your job? Rate it from 1 (unsatisfying) to 10 (highly satisfying) according to the following factors and then total your score:
   ___ brings meaning and purpose to my life
   ___ allows me to control my own work pace
   ___ few drastic, job-threatening consequences if I fail
   ___ little spillover from work into leisure time
   ___ Total score

4. In which of the following areas of life do you find your greatest sense of purpose?
   - ❏ work
   - ❏ parenting
   - ❏ church
   - ❏ marriage
   - ❏ community work
   - ❏ being a friend
   - ❏ creative self-expression
   - ❏ working on political issues

INTRODUCTION TO THE BIBLE STUDY

Jesus delivered his most important sermon from a mountainside. Because of his fame, he could not enter a city without drawing huge crowds and the watchful eye of the religious leaders who opposed him. So for most of three years, Jesus walked along the countryside ministering and preaching about the kingdom of God. From his illustrations in this so-called "Sermon on the Mount" (Matthew 5–7), it is clear that Jesus was careful to observe and learn many spiritual lessons from the world around him. Though his mind was on the future kingdom (his purpose), his eyes were constantly noticing all of life around him—birds of the air, lilies of the field, fig trees and the natural signs of seasonal changes.

In this passage, Jesus points out that if we give our life the proper focus—on the kingdom of God—then the other things that worry us will fall in line as surely as they are provided for in nature. Birds and flowers thrive without all the work and anxiety humans go through. These words probably had even more relevance when Jesus spoke them. Having enough food and clothing to survive was much more uncertain in those days than it is in most industrialized countries today.

ICE-BREAKER FOR TWO-SESSION OPTION
If you are doing the Bible Study as a separate session, start off this session by dividing this group into subgroups of 4 to 6 and answering the following questions. Photocopy and give this to the group.

---

1. What was your most frightful experience of nature?
   - ❏ hurricane
   - ❏ blizzard
   - ❏ hailstorm
   - ❏ lightning
   - ❏ tornado
   - ❏ flood
   - ❏ typhoon
   - ❏ other:_____

2. Which of the following places or acts of nature would help you feel closest to God? Explain why.
   - ❏ the ocean
   - ❏ a (rain) forest
   - ❏ a waterfall
   - ❏ a sunny day
   - ❏ a mountain
   - ❏ a mountain stream
   - ❏ a thunderstorm
   - ❏ other:_____

SESSION FOUR BIBLE STUDY

²⁵*"Therefore I tell you, do not worry about your life, what you will eat or drink; or about your body, what you will wear. Is not life more important than food, and the body more important than clothes?* ²⁶*Look at the birds of the air; they do not sow or reap or store away in barns, and yet your heavenly Father feeds them. Are you not much more valuable than they?* ²⁷*Who of you by worrying can add a single hour to his life?*

²⁸*"And why do you worry about clothes? See how the lilies of the field grow. They do not labor or spin.* ²⁹*Yet I tell you that not even Solomon in all his splendor was dressed like one of these.* ³⁰*If that is how God clothes the grass of the field, which is here today and tomorrow is thrown into the fire, will he not much more clothe you, O you of little faith?* ³¹*So do not worry, saying, 'What shall we eat?' or 'What shall we drink?' or 'What shall we wear?'* ³²*For the pagans run after all these things, and your heavenly Father knows that you need them.* ³³*But seek first his kingdom and his righteousness, and all these things will be given to you as well.* ³⁴*Therefore do not worry about tomorrow, for tomorrow will worry about itself. Each day has enough trouble of its own."*

Matthew 6:25–34

1. What point is Jesus making about the birds? About the lilies of the field?

2. Which one of the following statements best reflects your view of the role of anxiety?
   ❏ A little anxiety keeps you on your toes.
   ❏ If you have faith, you should never worry.
   ❏ If you've never worried, you're simply not aware!
   ❏ You can't just stop worrying by wanting to stop.
   ❏ Worrying doesn't change the situation, so why worry?
   ❏ Faith helps us manage, not eliminate, anxiety.

3. Which of these is your main source of worry right now?
   ❏ what we will eat and wear—meeting my family's basic needs
   ❏ storing away in barns—saving for the future
   ❏ having "barns"—paying for real estate
   ❏ adding a single hour to my life—staying healthy
   ❏ maintaining the "splendor of Solomon"—paying for the extras we want
   ❏ something not mentioned here—heavy debt!

4. Jesus promises that if we "seek first his kingdom and his righteousness," our needs will be provided for. What must happen in order for you to lay claim to this promise in a deeper way?
   ❏ I need to believe the promise.
   ❏ I need to focus my life more on the kingdom of God.
   ❏ I need to see it work for someone else.
   ❏ I need to have this group's support in committing myself to the kingdom.
   ❏ I need to take a look at what my "needs" really are.
   ❏ other:_____

REFERENCE NOTES

Matthew 6:25–34

6:25 *do not worry.* Worry is a state of mind. Having chosen God's way, the Christian must not be overly concerned about the demands and pressures that occupy those committed to the other way (materialism).

6:26 The point is that since God provides for the needs of birds, will he not also provide for the needs of those whom he has created in his image (Gen. 1:26)? It is not that the birds don't have to do anything for their food, but rather that they get it without the stress and anxiety we often feel we have to go through.

6:27 Worry is unable to accomplish anything. In fact, because worry brings on health problems, it is more likely to subtract from our span of life.

6:28–30 Building on his comment in verse 25, Jesus encourages his followers to consider how even flowers, unable to rush about in anxious pursuit of their physical needs, are adorned with beauty. Since God provides them with such beauty, why should his people fear that they will be neglected by God?

6:29 *Solomon.* Solomon, the third king of Israel, was noted for his fabulous wealth (1 Kings 10:14–29). The folly of being anxious about clothing is seen in that even the simplest flower (including many weeds that were only used as fuel—v. 30) is adorned more delicately and attractively than the richest man or woman.

6:30 *you of little faith.* As the two illustrations here show, faith is reliance on the love, care and power of God. Faith is the opposite of anxiety.

thrown into the fire. People used dry flowers and grass as fuel in their ovens. God cares for every aspect of his creation, regardless of how long it lasts, but he has special concern for those whom he has created for eternal fellowship.

6:31 *What shall we eat / drink / wear?* This is the "world's Trinity of cares" (Stott).

6:33 The attention of Jesus' disciples is to be focused on doing God's work ("his kingdom") and imitating his character ("his righteousness"). The supreme ambition of the Christian is to give glory to God in all of his or her thoughts, words and actions.

6:34 *tomorrow.* Worry generally has to do with the future, about what lies ahead. The disciple is to live one day at a time and leave the future in God's hands.

trouble. Disciples are not promised a trouble-free life: they are promised God's care. Everyone experiences stress. But if we limit our stress to that which we face today, then we are more likely to keep it manageable.

CARING TIME

Close by sharing prayer requests and by taking time to pray for one another. Remember the sources of worry that were expressed during the meeting. Begin by having each group member answer the question:

"How can we help you in prayer this week?"

Conclude your prayer time by reading Psalm 34:17-19 together:

The righteous cry out, and the Lord hears them;
he delivers them from all their troubles.
The Lord is close to the brokenhearted
and saves those who are crushed in spirit.

A righteous man may have many troubles,
but the Lord delivers him from them all.

LEADER:

If applicable, have the group use the extra space on this page for group prayer requests.

SESSION 5

Just Say "Thanks"

OBJECTIVES

To see how we add stress to our life when, instead of being thankful for what we have, we focus on what we don't have.

To consider what we have to be thankful for, both materially and in terms of our accomplishments.

To find how Paul's learning to be "content whatever the circumstances" can help us today.

THREE-PART AGENDA

ICE-BREAKER
15 Minutes

ISSUE / BIBLE STUDY
45 Minutes

CARING TIME
30 Minutes

OPTION: If you only have 60 minutes, divide this session into two sessions, with the Bible Study section for your next time together.

ICE-BREAKER

Pass out the Handout for this session or the course book to each person. Divide the group into subgroups of 4 to 6 to do the Ice-Breaker. (Photocopy pages 41 and 43 as needed.)

1. When you eat a meal at a restaurant, what are you more likely to do?
   ❏ eat quickly and then look for more
   ❏ savor every bite
   ❏ eat everything with pleasure, and then feel guilty
   ❏ pick at my food and then leave half of it on the plate
   ❏ notice how much better someone else's order looks
   ❏ other:_____

2. What is your favorite "gourmet" life experience?
   ❏ watching sunsets
   ❏ talking with friends late into the night
   ❏ eating expensive chocolates
   ❏ taking a leisurely bubble bath or relaxing in the jacuzzi
   ❏ having breakfast in bed
   ❏ taking a drive in a convertible on a sunny day
   ❏ other:_____

INTRODUCTION TO THE ISSUE

LEADER:

• Summarize these remarks (in your own words) into a brief introduction (no longer than 5 minutes).

• Be careful not to read the entire presentation to the group.

• In your presentation cover the "Discuss the Issue" questions listed on Side One of the Handout.

Philosopher-writer Sam Keen says most people feel like exiles, living far from the "homeland,"—the place in life where they really want to be. People will continue to feel emotionally distant, he says, until they realize they have been "riding on an ox, looking for an ox," until they look at and appreciate where they already are, what is right there under their feet. The process of coming to that awareness, he says, is our "homecoming."[15]

Stress researcher Hans Selye believes that this discontent with what we have and what we have accomplished is a major factor in stress. He writes:

"... among people engaged in the most common occupations of modern society ... one of the major sources of distress arises from dissatisfaction with life, namely, from disrespect from their own accomplishments."[16]

Doesn't it stand to reason that not being thankful for what we have and what we have accomplished would be stressful? It's like running with a carrot forever dangling out in front of us, but never reaching it. Whatever we have, whatever we do, it's never enough. "More" drives our life. We have to get more. We have to do more. When John D. Rockefeller was asked how much money it takes to satisfy a person he said, "Just a little more." The same could be said by those of us driven by accomplishment. The frustration which comes from never reaching what we are striving for is a tremendous cause of stress.

Turning discontent into thanksgiving is, then, a necessary part of managing stress. This is a three-step process:

• Taking inventory of what we have, not what we don't have.
• Replacing negative life-statements with positive life-statements.
• Letting ourselves be joyful.

Taking inventory of what we have

The old song advises us, "Count your blessings, name them one by one; Count your many blessings, see what God hath done." That is still good advice! Too often we only think about what we don't have. Author and minister John Claypool believes this is not just a recent phenomenon, either. He sees the story of Adam and Eve as a situation where God set a banquet before them and they grasped for more.[17]

Evan

For a long time, Evan was "working his tail off" and "getting nowhere financially." He had no savings. He barely had enough money to cover expenses, with nothing left for "extras." For every bill he paid, another one would take its place. But then Evan was led to take a more complete inventory of his life. He and his family had in fact made a lot of progress, but he had not really noticed. Five years earlier his debt had been building at the rate of $400 a month. Now his debt level was keeping stable. The family was living in a nicer home and had been able to obtain some luxuries which Evan had not really taken note of (such as a video camera). In addition, Evan remembered that he now had some nonmaterial blessings which he had not duly shown thanks for, including a healthy three-year-old daughter he didn't have five years earlier, as well as a more satisfying job. Evan concluded that he had been focusing only on what was not happening in his life.

Choosing positive life statements

After taking inventory of what we have going for us, we then need to start choosing to make positive statements about our life, instead of only negative statements. Clinical psychologist Martin Shaffer writes, "Many events remain stressors for us only because we continually remind ourselves about them. ... Thus, each negative statement functions as a specific stressor."[18]

Such negative statements are often a big factor in spiritual stresses. "Why doesn't God help me with this problem?" "Why doesn't God answer this question?" We fail to stop and ask why God has blessed us with all of the things we do have, and why he has helped us find the strength to overcome the problems we have had. The country song of several years ago asked, "Why me, Lord? What have I ever done to deserve even one of the pleasures I've known?"

Clarisse decided after a period of financial stress to start including in her prayers each night a deliberate time to thank God for every blessing she received that day. She found that this discipline made her life seem much less stressful.

Letting ourselves be joyful

It may seem a strange thing to say that we need to let ourselves be joyful. Why would anyone not want to be joyful? But sometimes we are the ones preventing it. We may feel at some level that being an adult means we have to be worried and overly concerned with responsibilities, and that if we are not, we are not taking our adult responsibilities seriously. Or it may be that we think we don't deserve joy. Whatever is the case, a life without joy is a stressful life. Author and minister Bruce Larson writes: "Our ability to accept happiness, or actually the courage to accept it, determines greatly how well we are physically and emotionally." He goes on to add, "The irresponsible person full of joy can often be healthier than the stressful, worried person who is a Puritan in diet and habit."[19] And Proverbs 17:22 says, "A cheerful heart is good medicine, but a crushed spirit dries up the bones."

What is the choice we are going to make about how we are going to live the rest of our life? Are we going to choose to focus on what we don't have and make negative statements about our life? Are we going to choose to yell and scream at God and everyone else because something hasn't gone as we thought it should? Or are we going to choose to be joyful, thanking God for what we have? The choice is up to us.

SESSION FIVE HANDOUT: Stress Management

Just Say "Thanks"

 ICE-BREAKER / Groups of 4 to 6 / 15 Minutes

1. When you eat a meal at a restaurant, what are you more likely to do?
   - ❐ eat quickly and then look for more
   - ❐ savor every bite
   - ❐ eat everything with pleasure, and then feel guilty
   - ❐ pick at my food and then leave half of it on the plate
   - ❐ notice how much better someone else's order looks
   - ❐ other:_____

2. What is your favorite "gourmet" life experience?
   - ❐ watching sunsets
   - ❐ talking with friends late into the night
   - ❐ eating expensive chocolates
   - ❐ taking a leisurely bubble bath or relaxing in the jacuzzi
   - ❐ having breakfast in bed
   - ❐ taking a drive in a convertible on a sunny day
   - ❐ other:_____

DISCUSS THE ISSUE / Same Groups / 20 Minutes

After a brief introduction by the leader, take turns sharing your responses to the following questions.

1. Why is it that so often we focus on what we don't have instead of what we do have?
   - ❐ We take what we have for granted.
   - ❐ It keeps us from becoming self-satisfied.
   - ❐ We're searching for something to make us happy, not realizing happiness does not come from things.
   - ❐ We're led to do so by Satan.
   - ❐ We are pushed that way by a consumer-oriented society.
   - ❐ I do it because I really am poor!
   - ❐ other:_____

2. When have you been like Evan—focused on what was *not* happening in your life? To what extent are you doing that now?

3. In one minute, share as many things as you can think of that God has blessed you with.

INTRODUCTION TO THE BIBLE STUDY

The book of Philippians was one of the last letters Paul wrote. He wrote it from a Roman jail, probably not long before his execution. Since he was undoubtedly aware of the danger before him, the joy and positive spirit of this letter is a very special witness to Paul's faith. He writes to the Philippian church as if he had a special relationship with them. Just recently they had sent a gift of support for him, and Paul took care to express his thanks. Paul did not complain about what he didn't have or about all the churches that did not send him help. He gave thanks for what he had, and for what had been given to him.

We do not want to idolize Paul here, for he was as human as we are. There most certainly were times when Paul did not feel the same way he did when he wrote this letter. But the insight shown here is one of the best examples of what God can do to give a person the spirit to face any situation with joy and hope. In times of stress, it is just that spirit we all need.

> **ICE-BREAKER FOR TWO-SESSION OPTION**
> *If you are doing the Bible Study as a separate session, start off this session by dividing this group into subgroups of 4 to 6 and answering the following questions. Photocopy and give this to the group.*

The things we longed for as a child tell us almost as much about ourselves as the possessions we cherished the most.

1. When you were in the fourth grade, which of the following would have been like a dream-come-true for you?
   ❏ finding a pirate's treasure
   ❏ getting a black stallion of my own
   ❏ having the biggest baseball card collection in my neighborhood
   ❏ having clothes that were nicer than any of the other kids
   ❏ finding out my family was moving into a mansion
   ❏ going on one of the "kid-week" game shows and winning
   ❏ having my parent(s) build our own swimming pool
   ❏ having my own tree house or fort
   ❏ I never even thought about such things.
   ❏ other:_____

2. When you were in the fourth grade, what did you consider to be your most prized possession? What made this possession special?

SESSION FIVE BIBLE STUDY

> *⁴Rejoice in the Lord always. I will say it again: Rejoice! ⁵Let your gentleness be evident to all. The Lord is near. ⁶Do not be anxious about anything, but in everything, by prayer and petition, with thanksgiving, present your requests to God. ⁷And the peace of God, which transcends all understanding, will guard your hearts and your minds in Christ Jesus. ...*
>
> *¹⁰I rejoice greatly in the Lord that at last you have renewed your concern for me. Indeed, you have been concerned, but you had no opportunity to show it. ¹¹I am not saying this because I am in need, for I have learned to be content whatever the circumstances. ¹²I know what it is to be in need, and I know what it is to have plenty. I have learned the secret of being content in any and every situation, whether well fed or hungry, whether living in plenty or in want. ¹³I can do everything through him who gives me strength.*
>
> Philippians 4:4–7,10–13

1. When Paul says to "rejoice in the Lord always," what do you think he means?
   - ❐ In all circumstances, rejoice that we have the Lord with us.
   - ❐ Rejoice even for tragedy, because God has willed it.
   - ❐ Find whatever there is to rejoice about in every situation.
   - ❐ Rejoice whenever we see God's will done.
   - ❐ Find every opportunity to share our joy over God's love.

2. Why does Paul, sitting in jail and facing a possible death sentence, deny that he is in need (v. 11)?
   - ❐ He was being macho.
   - ❐ He didn't want to worry the Philippians.
   - ❐ Truly great Christians don't need anyone or anything but God.
   - ❐ He had put all the things people think they need in their proper perspective.
   - ❐ He had learned that with Christ he could be content in all circumstances.
   - ❐ As bad as the situation was, he had gotten used to it.

3. What is the difference between "being content whatever the circumstances" and being complacent? How can you illustrate this in your own life?

4. For you to find contentment, what do you most need to do right now?
   - ❐ stop focusing on the material
   - ❐ remember what Christ has done for me
   - ❐ remember in my losses how much I still have
   - ❐ trust God in the midst of what I fear I might lose
   - ❐ be thankful for what God has helped me accomplish
   - ❐ focus on the joys of the present moment
   - ❐ remember that the greatest joy is knowing Christ

REFERENCE NOTES

Philippians 4:4–7,10–13

4:4 ***Rejoice in the Lord.*** Faith "in the Lord" makes joyfulness both realistic and possible despite persecution and trouble.

4:6 ***prayer / petition / requests.*** Paul uses three synonyms to describe the alternative to anxiety.

with thanksgiving. "Thanksgiving means giving God the glory in everything, making room for him, casting our care on him, letting it be his care" (Barth).

4:7 ***the peace of God.*** This is the peace that characterizes God's inner character. It is this peace which he offers to share with his children. Such peace can never be figured out or produced by people themselves.

4:10 ***that ... you have been concerned.*** The cause of his rejoicing is not the gift, *per se,* but the concern that the believers showed for him.

at last. Apparently the Philippians had not been in contact with Paul for quite some time. Paul was aware that the church had gone through some hard times, and hadn't had the opportunity to help him.

4:11 Paul was not in difficult straits financially. He accepted their gift only because it was of great benefit to them to give in this way (see vv. 17–18).

content. Paul borrows this word from the vocabulary of the Stoic philosophers, who used it to describe the person who was self-sufficient and able to exist without anything or anyone. However, Paul's sufficiency is found in the Lord. Paul didn't teach from "an ivory tower." He had been through a lot in his life: he had been persecuted, shipwrecked, and robbed while in the service of the Lord. There had been times when he had plenty of food and personal support, and there had been times he had been without either. These had taught Paul a lesson—how to accept and adjust to the changes of life.

4:12 ***need.*** This refers to the fundamental needs which are basic to life, such as food and water. Paul has learned to exist even in the midst of poverty.

plenty. Literally, "to overflow." This is to have enough for one's own needs plus something left over.

4:13 ***everything.*** A better translation of this word would be "all these things." Paul is referring to what he has just described: his ability to exist in all types of material circumstances—wealth or poverty, abundant food or no food, etc.

through him who gives me strength. The "secret" (v. 12) Paul has learned which enables him to live with contentment in all circumstances is his union with Christ (see also 2 Cor. 12:9–10).

CARING TIME

Begin by sharing personal prayer requests and then answering the question:

"What difficult circumstances do you need God's strength to help you deal with right now?"

Take turns praying for each other remembering the requests and concerns that have been shared. Close by taking a few minutes for each group member to say a brief prayer of thanksgiving for the blessings that God has graciously and lovingly bestowed upon them.

LEADER:

If applicable, have the group use the extra space on this page for group prayer requests.

SESSION 6

A Little Help From My Friends

OBJECTIVES

To consider the stress which comes from relationships, and important factors in managing that stress.

To discuss how the presence of supportive friends is a necessary part of stress management.

To look at the story of Jesus in Gethsemane, and what it says about stress and friendship.

THREE-PART AGENDA

| ICE-BREAKER | ISSUE / BIBLE STUDY | CARING TIME |
| 15 Minutes | 45 Minutes | 30 Minutes |

OPTION: If you only have 60 minutes, divide this session into two sessions, with the Bible Study section for your next time together.

ICE-BREAKER

Pass out the Handout for this session or the course book to each person. Divide the group into subgroups of 4 to 6 to get acquainted by doing the Ice-Breaker. (Photocopy pages 49 and 51 as needed.)

1. Who was your best friend in junior high (grades 7–8), and how did you become good friends?

2. With whom do you have the longest-standing friendship right now? To what do you give credit for how long this relationship has lasted?

3. Considering your friendship history, what would you say is most important to you in a friend?
   - ❏ common interests
   - ❏ sense of humor
   - ❏ honesty
   - ❏ loyalty
   - ❏ accepting, doesn't judge
   - ❏ speaks his/her mind
   - ❏ shares my faith
   - ❏ willing to listen
   - ❏ commitment
   - ❏ openness
   - ❏ spends time with me
   - ❏ spontaneous
   - ❏ other:_____

INTRODUCTION TO THE ISSUE

LEADER:

• Summarize these remarks (in your own words) into a brief introduction (no longer than 5 minutes).

• Be careful not to read the entire presentation to the group.

• In your presentation cover the "Discuss the Issue" questions listed on Side One of the Handout.

When it comes to handling stress, almost nothing beats a good friend. A friend listens and helps us to "let off steam," provides an objective opinion when we aren't sure how to handle a situation, and helps us laugh and to "look on the bright side." With all of these benefits, it's unfortunate that so many of us don't have friends we can turn to in need. This is especially true of men. By the estimates of some psychologists and therapists, as few as 10 percent of American men have close friendships.[20]

If we find that we do not have an adequate friendship support system, we need to become more intentional about building and maintaining such a system. That means making an ongoing effort to develop friendships that will be there for us over time. Alan Loy McGinnis, in his book, *The Friendship Factor,* points out five ways to build such friendships.

- **Give friendships priority**—Friendships take time, and to have friendships that are worthwhile we have to give them priority. That may mean putting aside work or a pet project in order to be with a friend.

- **Be open**—To have friends we must be willing to honestly disclose who we are.

- **Show affection**—Don't be afraid to verbalize your caring, and show it in appropriate forms of physical affection, like hugging.

- **Put love into action**—Don't just talk about how you feel: show it by helping your friend with projects or by giving your friend little gifts.

- **Be nonpossessive**—Develop other friendships and allow your friend to do the same.[21]

Overcoming fear of relationships

As important as the above factors are, there is one which perhaps precedes them—do not be afraid to develop close relationships. Some of us fear intimacy because we know that relationships can often be stressful. We think that we have all the stress we can handle, and we prefer to play it safe when it comes to friendships. We may think, "If I don't get close to people, I cannot get hurt when they fail or abandon me."

We fail to recognize what we lose. Not only do we lose the strength friendships can give in times of stress, but we also miss the learning opportunity which conflict can provide. Author John Claypool writes, "Just as friction between certain types of rocks produces sparks of light, so the friction of one individual personality rubbing against another produces sparks that illuminate what each one is truly like."[22] We learn more of what we are like by seeing how others react to us—including how some of our behavior may irritate them!

Types of stressful relationships

We can learn from stress in relationships, but we also want to learn how to manage stress so our relationships can be more positive. This requires us to understand the different types of stressful relationships:

- **Unresolved conflict**—Relationships become stressful when people don't deal with their problems. This especially happens if we overvalue the idea of "keeping things pleasant." We don't like to fight and so we keep our mouths shut.

Ward

Ward found himself suffering from the effects of stress because of his inability to confront conflict in his marriage. He was in his final year of graduate school (which was stressful in itself) and was getting upset over what he thought was the increasingly critical attitude of his wife. Rather than talking about his feelings, however, he repressed them and just tried harder to please her. Soon they began to have sexual difficulties, and once again Ward didn't share his feelings, except to complain mildly from time to time. By the end of the school year, Ward was suffering from palpitations, muscle spasms in his chest, and an intense fear that he was going to have a heart attack.

Dealing with stress from conflict means learning to share our feelings regularly with the people we want to be closest to us. Only by doing so do we keep stress from mounting.

- **Trauma**—The death of a loved one, being abused, rejected, or abandoned, or some kind of trauma from a past relationship can bring stress to present relationships and make us unable to relate to people.

Alice

For five years, Alice had kept secret the fact that she had been raped by her brother-in-law. She had never told anyone about it because of the shame she felt, and because she didn't want to bring stress to the family. But as a result, she had difficulty sleeping, suffered frequent headaches, and felt very uncomfortable around men.

In situations where a past trauma is disrupting our present relationships, we should consult a counselor and try to deal with our past pain. Only when that pain is confronted and dealt with can we find relationships that are full and satisfying.

- **Overinvolvement**—Sometimes relationships can be stressful because we are overinvolved in them emotionally. Every problem another person has becomes our problem. We may be weighted down because our best friend is getting divorced, or our sister is having difficulty with a pregnancy, or someone at work has a sick child. Some people even get upset because of the difficulties of a character on their favorite soap opera!

Relationships do cause stress—there's no doubt about that. But healthy relationships also provide a vital resource for managing the stress in all areas of our lives. If we can keep these friendships in perspective (and not become entangled by them), then we will indeed "get by with a little help from our friends."

SESSION SIX HANDOUT: Stress Management

A Little Help From My Friends

 ICE-BREAKER / Groups of 4 to 6 / 15 Minutes

1. Who was your best friend in junior high (grades 7–8), and how did you become good friends?

2. With whom do you have the longest-standing friendship right now? To what do you give credit for how long this relationship has lasted?

3. Considering your friendship history, what would you say is most important to you in a friend?
   - ❏ common interests
   - ❏ sense of humor
   - ❏ honesty
   - ❏ loyalty
   - ❏ accepting, doesn't judge
   - ❏ speaks his/her mind
   - ❏ shares my faith
   - ❏ willing to listen
   - ❏ commitment
   - ❏ openness
   - ❏ spends time with me
   - ❏ spontaneous
   - ❏ other:_____

DISCUSS THE ISSUE / Same Groups / 20 Minutes
After a brief introduction by the leader, take turns sharing your responses to the following questions.

1. What would you say is the biggest factor that keeps us from having good friendships today?
   - ❏ fear of being intimate
   - ❏ hectic work schedules
   - ❏ People are always moving.
   - ❏ Everyone's too competitive.
   - ❏ TV—It keeps us home!
   - ❏ Everyone focuses on themselves.
   - ❏ Fewer people are joining church and social organizations.

2. Of McGinnis' ways of developing friendships, which one is most difficult for you?
   - ❏ making friendship a priority
   - ❏ being open about myself
   - ❏ showing affection
   - ❏ finding ways to show I care
   - ❏ not being possessive

3. What needs to be your next step in developing healthy relationships?
   - ❏ admit how much I need people
   - ❏ learn that I also have my part to contribute
   - ❏ believe that having friends relieves more stress than it creates
   - ❏ learn I cannot please everyone
   - ❏ learn that rejection isn't fatal
   - ❏ learn that there are people who accept me

INTRODUCTION TO THE BIBLE STUDY

The story of Jesus in Gethsemane, perhaps more than any other story in the New Testament, clearly shows Jesus' humanity. In his humanity he suffered, and in his suffering he wanted friendship and support. Over the three-year period of his ministry he had developed some friendships, particularly with those we call the 12 disciples. They had traveled together, eaten together and bared their souls to each other. They were Jesus' support group. Just before this story begins, they had shared together in the "Last Supper," where their fellowship had centered around the partaking of the symbols of Christ's body and blood.

Within this group, there were three whom Jesus seemed to trust and rely on more than the others—Peter, James and John. It is these three whom he asks to come and be with him in his hour of agony. In Gethsemane, a garden on the Mount of Olives just outside of Jerusalem, Jesus wrestled with his purpose and the prospect of the suffering he was going to face. He asked Peter, James and John to come with him and pray. What were they to pray for? Was it for their own strength? That was certainly part of it. But they also were to lend their prayers to strengthen Jesus and support him in his time of stress. If Jesus sought the presence and support of friends during difficult times, how much more should we? Jesus' friends failed him on this occasion—they fell asleep. But it is probable that from this failure they learned a valuable lesson on how to support people. From this core group developed the house churches which stuck together in the midst of intense persecution, so that the family of God could thrive and grow. We have the opportunity to learn from both their failure and their success.

ICE-BREAKER FOR TWO-SESSION OPTION
If you are doing the Bible Study as a separate session, start off this session by dividing this group into subgroups of 4 to 6 and answering the following questions. Photocopy and give this to the group.

---

1. Which of the following famous friendships reminds you of a friendship of your own?
   ❑ Snoopy and Woodstock (from *Peanuts*)—We have a lot of silent understandings.
   ❑ The Lone Ranger and Tonto—We can always trust each other.
   ❑ Felix and Oscar (*The Odd Couple*)—We have little if anything in common, but we like each other!
   ❑ "The Honeymooners"—a friendship with another couple where we share and argue like family
   ❑ Norm and Cliff on *Cheers*—someone to hang out with, watch sports with, and give a hard time to
   ❑ Mary and Rhoda (*The Mary Tyler Moore Show*)—someone who drops by, and with whom I can talk about anything.

2. Which type of friendship above would you like to have more of?

SESSION SIX BIBLE STUDY

> ³⁶*Then Jesus went with his disciples to a place called Gethsemane, and he said to them, "Sit here while I go over there and pray." ³⁷He took Peter and the two sons of Zebedee along with him, and he began to be sorrowful and troubled. ³⁸Then he said to them, "My soul is overwhelmed with sorrow to the point of death. Stay here and keep watch with me."*
>
> ³⁹*Going a little farther, he fell with his face to the ground and prayed, "My Father, if it is possible, may this cup be taken from me. Yet not as I will, but as you will."*
>
> ⁴⁰*Then he returned to his disciples and found them sleeping. "Could you men not keep watch with me for one hour?" he asked Peter. ⁴¹"Watch and pray so that you will not fall into temptation. The spirit is willing, but the body is weak."*
>
> ⁴²*He went away a second time and prayed, "My Father, if it is not possible for this cup to be taken away unless I drink it, may your will be done."*
>
> ⁴³*When he came back, he again found them sleeping, because their eyes were heavy. ⁴⁴So he left them and went away once more and prayed the third time, saying the same thing.*
>
> ⁴⁵*Then he returned to the disciples and said to them, "Are you still sleeping and resting? Look, the hour is near, and the Son of Man is betrayed into the hands of sinners. ⁴⁶Rise, let us go! Here comes my betrayer!"*
>
> Matthew 26:36–46

1. Why do you think Jesus took Peter, James and John with him?
   - ❏ He wanted them on the lookout.
   - ❏ He needed their support.
   - ❏ He wanted them to pray for him.
   - ❏ He was testing their endurance.
   - ❏ He knew they needed to pray for themselves.

2. If you were Jesus and your friends fell asleep on you, what would you have done?
   - ❏ thrown cold water on them
   - ❏ excused their behavior—They were tired.
   - ❏ figured I wasn't worth worrying about
   - ❏ showed my anger through sarcasm
   - ❏ realized that everyone is out for themselves
   - ❏ expressed my anger clearly, but then let it slide
   - ❏ decided I was wrong to trust people to help me
   - ❏ other:_____

3. If you were to go through a time of agony like Jesus did in Gethsemane, what three friends (outside of persons in this group) would you choose to be with you?

4. What do you need to do to have friends who can support you in times of stress (instead of adding to your stress)?
   - ❏ choose my friends more carefully
   - ❏ learn to trust again
   - ❏ accept my friends' failings, as Jesus did
   - ❏ learn to support others myself
   - ❏ take time to develop such friendships
   - ❏ other:_____
   - ❏ become more open, especially about the stresses in my life

REFERENCE NOTES

Matthew 26:36–46

26:36 *Gethsemane.* This was an olive orchard in an estate at the foot of the Mount of Olives, just outside the eastern wall of Jerusalem. The name literally means "an oil press" (for making olive oil). Jesus asks most of the disciples to sit and wait and then invites Peter, James and John to go with him further.

26:38 *overwhelmed with sorrow to the point of death.* Many people have speculated about what Jesus meant. Certainly he faced the wrath and punishment of God in bearing the sins of humankind. He may also have felt overwhelmed by any number of the following: concern that he might give in to temptation and forego the cross; worry over what his disciples would do without him; hesitancy to let go of this life.

keep watch. Jesus was simply asking them to keep him company and give him support by their presence and prayers.

26:39 *fell.* Jesus' prayer posture here shows both his agony and his submission to God. Like Job (in chapter 1), Jesus "fell with his face to the ground." Jesus' emotions showed his humanity, while his words and actions showed his complete obedience to the will of God.

prayed. He would have prayed aloud, as was the custom for people at the time, so the disciples heard (and remembered) his prayer.

My Father. This was not a title for God that was used in prayer in the first century. It expressed an intimacy that would have been considered inappropriate.

this cup. In the Old Testament, drinking a cup of bitter wine was often used as a symbol for experiencing God's judgment (e.g., Ps. 75:8; Isa. 51:17–22). By this image Jesus refers to the events of his death that are fast coming upon him.

Yet not as I will, but as you will. This phrase, popularly used today as a generalized "escape clause" when people are unsure what to pray, is actually an affirmation of Jesus' intent to pursue the Father's will even when he did not like it. As the repeated predictions of his death indicate, there was no doubt in Jesus' mind regarding what the Father's will was in this situation. While he pleads that there might be another way, this sentence declares his commitment to follow the Father's lead regardless of the cost (see also v. 42).

26:41 *The spirit is willing, but the body is weak.* The "spirit" probably refers to the human spirit energized by God. The problem is that the disciples allowed their physical condition to dictate their response to an impending spiritual crisis. They should have prepared themselves for the danger that lay ahead.

CARING TIME

Take time now to share any personal prayer requests. This meeting may have brought up some positive and negative situations with relationships. Use this time to pray for one another in light of the feelings and concerns that have been shared. Go around the group and have each person pray for the person on their left. Start with this sentence:

"Dear God, I want to talk with you about my friend _____."

Conclude your prayer time by reading 1 John 4:7-12 together:

*Dear friends, let us love one another, for love comes from God.
Everyone who loves has been born of God and knows God.
Whoever does not love does not know God, because God is love.
This is how God showed his love among us:
He sent his one and only Son into the world
that we might live through him.*

*This is love: not that we loved God, but that he loved us
and sent his Son as an atoning sacrifice for our sins.
Dear friends, since God so loved us,
we also ought to love one another.
No one has ever seen God; but if we love one another,
God lives in us and his love is made complete in us.*

LEADER:

If applicable, have the group use the extra space on this page for group prayer requests.

SESSION 7

Restoring the Soul

OBJECTIVES

To see how going beyond human resources to draw on the resources of God can greatly increase our capacity to manage stress.

To consider methods of prayer and meditation.

To examine Psalm 23 as a scriptural resource for helping us to deal with stress.

THREE-PART AGENDA

 **ISSUE / BIBLE STUDY** 45 Minutes

 **ICE-BREAKER** 15 Minutes

 **CARING TIME** 30 Minutes

NOTE: The agenda is reversed and there is no two-session option.

ICE-BREAKER

NOTE:
Ice-Breaker goes last with Evaluation / Caring Time.

We recommend that you use the Ice-Breaker at the close of this session—as part of the Evaluation / Caring time. This affirmation exercise is on the back of the Handout.

You have had a chance to observe the gifts and talents of the members of your group. Now, you will have a chance to pass out some much deserved praise for the contribution that each member of the group has made to your life. Read out loud the first award. Then, let everyone nominate the person they feel is the most deserving for that award. Then read the next award, etc., through the list. Have fun!

SPARK PLUG: The person who ignited the group.

DEAR ABBY AWARD: The person who cared enough to listen.

ROYAL GIRDLE AWARD: The person who supported us.

WINNIE THE POOH AWARD: The warm, caring person when someone needed a hug.

ROCK OF GIBRALTER AWARD: The person who was strong in the tough times of our group.

OPRAH AWARD: The person who asked the fun questions that got us to talk.

more ⟶

TED KOPPEL AWARD: The person who asked the heavy questions that made us think.

KING ARTHUR'S AWARD: The knight in shining armor who saved damsels in distress.

PINK PANTHER AWARD: The detective who made us deal with Scripture.

TRAFFIC COP AWARD: The person who went out of their way to keep order in the meetings.

BIG MAC AWARD: The person who showed great hunger for spiritual things.

SERENDIPITY CROWN: The person who grew the most spiritually during the course (in your estimation).

INTRODUCTION TO THE ISSUE

LEADER:

• Summarize these remarks (in your own words) into a brief introduction (no longer than 5 minutes).

• Be careful not to read the entire presentation to the group.

• In your presentation cover the "Discuss the Issue" questions listed on Side One of the Handout.

The story is told of a man who made a trip with some tribal people along the Amazon River. He was anxious to continue the trek, but was surprised when he found the natives seated together and doing nothing. When he asked the reason for the delay, the leader explained: "They are waiting. They cannot move farther until their souls have caught up with their bodies."

Some of us may chuckle at the simple notion of these tribal people. Others may be quick to point out an error in their theology. But the fact is, at least they knew they had souls that needed to be cared for! That's more than can be said for many people in our society today! In a world where so many of us rush around (like "chickens with our heads cut off"), there is an element of truth that "our souls have not caught up with our bodies."

Matters of the soul have always been a concern of the religious. That is to be expected. It is, after all, their business. But more and more we find a similar concern being expressed by secular professionals, as they see meditation and "spiritual growth" as an important part of stress management even for the nonreligious.

Religious and secular authorities may agree on the spiritual nature of the problem. They may also "prescribe" similar methods—such as meditation—for handling stress and its effect on the soul. But they have significant differences over the question of what the spiritual focus of our lives should be.

"Is my life focused primarily on myself, or is my focus on Jesus Christ?" That is the crucial question each of us must ask. It is an outrageous demand, when you think about it! To bow down to one person as if he were a king and to promise to live according to his rules seems so alien to us. If Jesus is not who he said he was, then it would be foolish. But if he is indeed God in human form as he claimed, then he would have the power to do everything he promised.

55

Spiritual disciplines

It is only after we have this spiritual focus on Christ that we can consider the methods for tending to the well-being of our souls. These spiritual disciplines include meditation, prayer, silence and solitude.

- **Meditation**

  Christian meditation is deep thinking about the things of God. That is what distinguishes it from other forms of meditation, such as Eastern religions and Transcendental Meditation. For the Christian, meditation is not merely an emptying of the mind in order to reduce stress or to gain new self-awareness. Rather, it is a conscious effort to turn our minds away from our concerns, and to focus on God's design, purpose and nature. The more we are able to see life as God sees it, the better we will be able to handle difficulty and disappointment.

  We can use different means of meditating. Many people read Scripture. Some reflect upon a hymn, a song, or a poem; others upon the writings of the saints. Some meditate on the nature of God as reflected in the world around us. Each sort of meditation can be a form of spiritual food. But ultimately it is God who feeds our souls.

- **Prayer**

  Prayer is conversation with God. That involves two aspects: we talk and we listen. We express our concerns to God, who encourages us to share from our hearts. But it is when we listen that God can direct us away from so much of what causes excess stress in life. It can also help us to have a deeper understanding of where our stress has come from. Mike made a list of words which made him feel stressful (like "judgment" and "belonging"). While focusing on each word, he asked in prayer, "Lord, what would you say to me about this?" He sorted through the thoughts which came to mind for God's direction, and found that doing this brought him more insight into himself than anything he had tried.

- **Silence and solitude**

  Even when it is not used for meditation, solitude can get us away from stresses and help us focus our thoughts. Silence, similarly, can get us away from words, which (in excess) can often cause confusion. The Bible reminds us, "Much dreaming and many words are meaningless. Therefore stand in awe of God" (Eccl. 5:7).

Psychiatrist Paul Tournier makes this comparison:

> "I see this complicated human machine as a great organ with all its registers, its stops, and its pipes. But according to who you put at the manuals to play it, you will get a frightening cacophony, or marvelous heavenly music!"[23]

Even the most devout person experiences stress. But some of us may be experiencing far more stress than necessary by failing to let the "organist" bring forth the music from our lives.

SESSION SEVEN HANDOUT: Stress Management

Restoring the Soul

📖 DISCUSS THE ISSUE (Groups of 4 to 6 / 20 Min.)

1. In the past week, when have you felt like you needed "your soul to catch up with your body"?

2. When are you most likely to find your best time alone?
   - ❏ in my office
   - ❏ driving to work
   - ❏ when the house is empty
   - ❏ only when I ask for help with responsibilities
   - ❏ late at night
   - ❏ early in the morning
   - ❏ getting exercise
   - ❏ never

3. What course of action do you feel would be most helpful to you in regard to the spiritual disciplines?
   - ❏ maintain a daily prayer time
   - ❏ get away periodically for a time of solitude
   - ❏ reestablish my whole relationship with God
   - ❏ listen more in my prayer time
   - ❏ No change is necessary.
   - ❏ other:_____

📖 RESPOND TO THE BIBLE STUDY (Same Groups / 20–25 Min.)

23 The LORD is my shepherd, I shall not be in want. ²He makes me lie down in green pastures, he leads me beside quiet waters, ³he restores my soul. He guides me in paths of righteousness for his name's sake. ⁴Even though I walk through the valley of the shadow of death, I will fear no evil, for you are with me; your rod and your staff, they comfort me. ⁵You prepare a table before me in the presence of my enemies. You anoint my head with oil; my cup overflows. ⁶Surely goodness and love will follow me all the days of my life, and I will dwell in the house of the LORD forever.   *Psalm 23*

1. When you hear of "green pastures" or "quiet waters," what place (where you have been) comes to mind?

2. What would it mean for you to be led by God in the midst of the stresses of your life?
   - ❏ FINANCIAL AID—"I shall not be in want."
   - ❏ RELEASE FROM WORKAHOLISM—"He makes me lie down in green pastures."
   - ❏ SPIRITUAL DIRECTION—"He guides me in paths of righteousness."
   - ❏ FREEDOM FROM FEAR—"Even though I walk through the valley of the shadow of death, I will fear no evil."
   - ❏ VOCATIONAL TRAINING—"Your rod and your staff, they comfort me."
   - ❏ FRIENDSHIP—"I will dwell in the house of the LORD forever."

3. How would it change your life if you really took the message of this Scripture seriously and were absolutely certain of its promises?

INTRODUCTION TO THE BIBLE STUDY

Psalm 23 is one of the best known, most loved passages in the Bible. Its words are relevant mostly to a rural, pastoral setting. It uses simple language. There are few flowery words. Why, then, has it been such an enduring favorite? Because it reassures us that no matter what kind of stress we face in life, God's watchcare will see us through. What other message is more needed in the midst of the kind of life we face? As you read this psalm, read it as if you were doing so for the first time, looking for its direction regarding your particular sources of stress.

REFERENCE NOTES

Psalm 23

23:1 *shepherd.* Just as the psalmist David was Israel's shepherd, God is a shepherd in the sense that he protects and provides for his flock, Israel. To refer to God as a shepherd was not unusual (other Near Eastern nations used it as well). What is unusual is that the psalmist claims God as his personal shepherd.

23:2 *green pastures.* In the desert landscape, a green meadow would provide relief and comfort for the sheep. These would recall the holy pasture (Ex. 15:13), which was the immediate goal of the Hebrews in their Exodus from Egypt (Craigie).

quiet waters. Literally, "waters of rest"; these may refer to "resting places by water" or to "waters that bring refreshment."

23:3 *restores my soul.* Literally, "brings back." Two different meanings are possible: If the image is one of bringing stray sheep back into the fold (Isa. 49:5), this would suggest spiritual repentance and renewal. If the image is of drinking "waters of rest," then the meaning may be more like "he calms down my soul." Kidner ties these two ideas together: "The retrieving or reviving of the sheep pictures the deeper renewal of the man of God, spiritually perverse or ailing as he may be."

for his name's sake. God's reputation is closely tied to the way he protects and provides for people, and in the manner they follow his ways.

23:4 *the shadow of death.* Can also be translated, "deep darkness," "very deep shadow," or "dark as death." Whether David is speaking of death or merely grave danger, the implication is that he can face the threat without fear because the Lord is his shepherd.

rod. A short club worn at the belt and used for defense.

staff. A walking stick, used for controlling and disciplining the sheep.

23:5–6 The imagery now shifts from God as shepherd to God as host. "To be God's guest is to be more than an acquaintance, invited for a day. It is to live with Him" (Kidner).

SESSION SEVEN AFFIRMATION AND EVALUATION

Restoring the Soul

 ICE-BREAKER / All Together / 45 Minutes (Total)

You have had a chance to observe the gifts and talents of the members of your group. Now, you will have a chance to pass out some much deserved praise for the contribution that each member of the group has made to your life. Read out loud the first award. Then, let everyone nominate the person they feel is the most deserving for that award. Then read the next award, etc., through the list. Have fun!

SPARK PLUG: The person who ignited the group.

DEAR ABBY AWARD: The person who cared enough to listen.

ROYAL GIRDLE AWARD: The person who supported us.

WINNIE THE POOH AWARD: The warm, caring person when someone needed a hug.

ROCK OF GIBRALTER AWARD: The person who was strong in the tough times of our group.

OPRAH AWARD: The person who asked the fun questions that got us to talk.

TED KOPPEL AWARD: The person who asked the heavy questions that made us think.

KING ARTHUR'S AWARD: The knight in shining armor who saved damsels in distress.

PINK PANTHER AWARD: The detective who made us deal with Scripture.

TRAFFIC COP AWARD: The person who went out of their way to keep order in the meetings.

BIG MAC AWARD: The person who showed great hunger for spiritual things.

SERENDIPITY CROWN: The person who grew the most spiritually during the course (in your estimation).

 EVALUATION / CARING TIME / 30 Minutes

Take a few minutes to review your experience and reflect. Go around on each question and share your answers. When you have finished with the questions, take time to share prayer requests and close in prayer.

1. When you first started this course, how were you feeling?
2. How did you feel about opening up and sharing yourself with this group?
3. What was one of the most significant things you learned?
4. What was the high point in this course for you?
5. What did you appreciate most about this group?

CONTINUATION

Do you want to continue as a group? If so, what do you need to improve? Finish the sentence:

"If I were to suggest one thing we could work on as a group, it would be ... "

MAKE A COVENANT

A covenant is a promise made to each other in the presence of God. Its purpose is to indicate your intention to make yourselves available to one another for the fulfillment of the purposes you share. In a spirit of prayer, work your way through the following sentences, trying to reach an agreement on each statement pertaining to your ongoing life together. Write out your covenant like a contract, stating your purpose, goals, and the ground rules for your group.

1. The purpose of our group will be:

2. Our goals will be:

3. We will meet for _____ weeks, after which we will decide if we wish to continue as a group.

4. We will meet from _____ to _____ and we will strive to start on time and end on time.

5. We will meet at _____ (place) or we will rotate from house to house.

6. We will agree to the following ground rules for our group (check):

   ❏ PRIORITY: While you are in the course, you give the group meetings priority.

   ❏ PARTICIPATION: Everyone participates and no one dominates.

   ❏ RESPECT: Everyone is given the right to their own opinion, and all questions are encouraged and respected.

   ❏ CONFIDENTIALITY: Anything that is said in the meeting is never repeated outside the meeting.

   ❏ EMPTY CHAIR: The group stays open to new people at every meeting.

☐ SUPPORT: Permission is given to call upon each other in time of need at any time.

☐ ACCOUNTABILITY: We agree to let the members of the group hold us accountable to the commitments which each of us make in whatever loving ways we decide upon.

☐ ADVICE-GIVING: Unsolicited advice is not allowed.

☐ MISSION: We agree to do everything in our power to start a new group as our mission.

CURRICULUM AND OTHER FELT NEED GROUP COURSES

Other courses in this series of FELT NEED GROUP COURSES are listed below. For more information about other group resources and possible direction, please contact your small group coordinator or SERENDIPITY at 1-800-525-9563 or visit us at: www.serendipityhouse.com.

DIVORCE RECOVERY: Picking Up the Pieces

HEALTHY RELATIONSHIPS: Living Within Defined Boundaries

PARENTING ADOLESCENTS: Easing the Way to Adulthood

12 STEPS: The Path to Wholeness

MARRIAGE ENRICHMENT: Making a Good Marriage Better

BLENDED FAMILIES: Yours, Mine, Ours

DEALING WITH GRIEF & LOSS: Hope in the Midst of Pain

RESOURCES FOR FURTHER STUDY

The *Serendipity Bible for Groups* contains a number of Questionnaire Bible Studies. Generally there is no "right" answer to these questions. The answers reflect your understanding and your experience. The name for this sort of small group exercise is relational Bible Study, since the focus is more on the people in the group than on delving deeply into the text. You can do more rigorous Bible Study by using the questions in the margin of the *Serendipity Bible for Groups*.

There are two courses on stress management outlined in the *Serendipity Bible for Groups* under the categories of Youth and Marketplace. In addition, what follows are 14 suggested studies—seven from the Old Testament and seven from the New Testament. While these questionnaire studies do not always focus directly on stress management, they all discuss some aspect of the topic. These studies are listed in the order in which they occur in the Bible, not in the order in which you will necessarily want to study them.

Studies From the Old Testament

1. The Call of Abram (Genesis 11:27–12:9)
   Focus on Abram's response to God's calling, and the resulting stressful changes for him and his wife.

2. Jacob Wrestles With God (Genesis 32:22–32)
   Focus on the spiritual stress in your own life as you look at Jacob's "wrestling" with God.

3. Bricks Without Straw (Exodus 5:1–21)
   Focus on the stress that the expectations of others can cause in your life.

4. Crossing the Sea (Exodus 14:5–31)
   Consider through this study how God has helped you through the "Red Seas" of your life.

5. God Uses Moses' Hands (Exodus 17:1–16)
   Explore how Moses dealt with the stress of leading the Israelites.

6. The Widow's Oil (2 Kings 4:1–7)
   Compare the way you handle financial stress to this widow's story.

7. The Image of Gold and the Fiery Furnace (Daniel 3:1–30)
   Compare the experience of Shadrach, Meshach and Abednego in the fiery furnace to your own experience in stressful times.

Studies From the New Testament

1. Jesus Heals a Paralytic (Mark 2:1–12)
   Explore how a paralytic was healed from the physical stress in his life with the help of some friends.

2. Jesus Calms the Storm (Mark 4:35–41)
   Focus on how Jesus can help you calm the "storms" in your life.

3. Jesus Feeds the Five Thousand (Mark 6:30–44)
   Focus on your need for balance between work, rest and responding to the needs of others.

4. At the Home of Martha and Mary (Luke 10:38–42)
   Examine your personality and the balance in your life by looking at this story about Martha and Mary.

5. Peter Disowns Jesus (Luke 22:54–62)
   Focus on the stress that results from personal failure.

6. On the Road to Emmaus (Luke 24:13–35)
   Focus on Christ's presence with you in times of spiritual struggles.

7. Paul's Vision in Corinth (Acts 18:5–17)
   Explore how Paul handled his emotions under pressure and how he found encouragement.

ENDNOTES:

[1] Hans Selye, *Stress Without Distress* (Philadelphia: J.B. Lippincott Co., 1974), p. 32.
[2] Leo Buscaglia, *Living, Loving and Learning* (Thorofare, N.J.: Charles B. Slack, Inc., 1982), p. 51.
[3] Hans Selye, *Stress Without Distress* (Philadelphia: J.B. Lippincott Co., 1974), pp. 28–29.
[4] John Claypool, *The Light Within You* (Waco, TX: Word, 1983), p. 105.
[5] Martin Shaffner, *Life After Stress* (New York: Plenum Press, 1982), p. 29.
[6] Bruce Larson, *There's a Lot More to Health Than Not Being Sick* (Waco, TX: Word Publishing, 1981), pp.109–110.
[7] John Claypool, *The Light Within You* (Waco, TX: Word, 1983), pp. 43–46.
[8] Hans Selye, *Stress Without Distress* (Philadelphia: J.B. Lippincott Co., 1974), p. 73.
[9] Ibid., p. 94.
[10] Ibid., p. 78.
[11] Martin Shaffer, *Life After Stress* (New York: Plenum Press, 1982), p. 27.
[12] Hans Selye, *Stress Without Distress* (Philadelphia: J.B. Lippincott Co., 1974), p. 80.
[13] Rollo May, *The Meaning of Anxiety* (New York: W.W. Norton & Co., 1977), pp. 376-377.
[14] Ibid., pp. 366-367.
[15] Quoted in John Claypool, *The Light Within You* (Waco, TX: Word, 1983), pp. 58–63.
[16] Hans Selye, *Stress Without Distress* (Philadelphia: J.B. Lippincott Co., 1974), pp. 78–79.
[17] John Claypool, *The Light Within You* (Waco, TX: Word, 1983), pp. 52–53.
[18] Martin Shaffer, *Life After Stress* (New York: Plenum Press, 1982), p. 13.
[19] Bruce Larson, *There's a Lot More to Health Than Not Being Sick* (Waco, TX: Word Publishing, 1981), pp.122–123.
[20] Alan Loy McGinnis, *The Friendship Factor* (Minneapolis, MN: Augsburg Publishing House, 1979), p. 11.
[21] Ibid., pp. 19–81.
[22] John Claypool, *The Light Within You* (Waco, TX: Word, 1983), p. 203.
[23] Paul Tournier, *The Violence Within* (San Francisco: Harper and Row, 1978), pp. 77–78.

PERSONAL NOTES